6 Ways
to Teach
the
6 Traits
of Writing

6 Ways to Teach the 6 Traits of Writing

by Betty Hollas

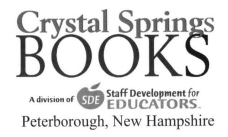

Crystal Springs
BOOKS

A division of **SDE** **Staff Development for EDUCATORS**

Peterborough, New Hampshire

Published by Crystal Springs Books
A division of Staff Development for Educators (SDE)
10 Sharon Road, PO Box 500
Peterborough, NH 03458
1-800-321-0401

www.crystalsprings.com
www.sde.com

Published 2006
Printed in the United States of America
10 09 08 07   2 3 4 5 6

ISBN-13: 978-1-884548-87-1

ISBN-10: 1-884548-87-3

Library of Congress Cataloging-in-Publication Data

Hollas, Betty, 1948-
  6 ways to teach the 6 traits of writing / by Betty Hollas.
      p. cm.
  Includes index.
  ISBN-13: 978-1-884548-87-1
  ISBN-10: 1-884548-87-3
  1. English language--Composition and exercises--Study and teaching (Elementary) 2.
Language arts (Elementary) I. Title: Six ways to teach the six traits of writing. II. Title.
  LB1576.H623 2006
  372.62'3--dc22

                    2006000936

Editor: Sharon Smith

Art Director, Designer, and Production Coordinator: Soosen Dunholter

To Jackson, who made me realize that when a baby is born, so is a grandmother!

Contents

Acknowledgments

Thank you to:

Sharon Smith, my editor for this book.

Soosen Dunholter, designer, art director, and production coordinator, who is responsible for making me look good.

Rebecca Mason, Senior Seminar Program Planner at Staff Development for Educators, who came up with the idea for this book.

Lorraine Walker, Staff Development for Educators Vice President of Publishing and New Product Development, who enthusiastically supported the idea from the beginning.

Deb Fredericks, Publishing Coordinator at Staff Development for Educators, for all her incredible behind-the-scenes work coordinating printers, publishing staff, and everyone else.

Jim Grant, Executive Director of Staff Development for Educators, speaker, author, and friend.

Char Forsten, Associate Executive Director of Staff Development for Educators, speaker, author, and friend. Char and I worked together to create the baseball rubrics in this book; Char also developed the CAPS strategy described on pages 59–60.

Melissa Hewson, fifth- and sixth-grade teacher in Phippsburg, Maine, for the ideas for Voice Sticks and "Show Me" Books on pages 34 and 31, respectively.

Madalyn Cooke, fifth- and sixth-grade teacher in The Woodlands, Texas, for the idea for the Wanted Posters for Vocabulary Words on page 35.

David Miller, teacher of grades nine through twelve in St. Charles, Missouri, for the idea for the consolidated version of the rubrics (pages 122–23).

Introduction

Why is writing so difficult to teach? I think I finally figured it out. Perhaps it's hard because you, as a teacher, may not see yourself as a writer. You probably see yourself as a *reader*, but not as a writer. So you end up *describing* the writing process to your students. I used to do that, and that's the traditional way.

This book will go way beyond the traditional way. Together we'll explore what's possible in your writing classroom by considering the traits or qualities of good writing and six ways you can weave these traits into your classroom writing instruction. This book is certainly not intended to be a comprehensive look at all the ways the traits of good writing could be part of a writing classroom. Nor is it intended to be followed strictly in one rigid sequence. Rather, I've provided an overview of the traits and have tried to give you lots of *choices* for ways you can use them with your student writers. I hope you'll feel free to pick and choose the strategies that will work best for you and—most important—for your students.

My goal is to empower you by suggesting ways you can enhance your writing curriculum. It is *not* to overwhelm you with more things you *have to* do. I promise: you will not feel that anything new is being added to your already full curriculum. I want to ease your burdens, not add to them.

You see, I struggled for so long trying to teach writing to my students, but for many years I instinctively relied on the way I was taught. Does that sound like something you can identify with? I would assign papers to my students. When I got the papers back, I would count the words and use my red pen. I would edit a lot for capitalization, grammar, punctuation, and spelling errors, and I would give very little feedback to help the student improve the *content* of a piece of writing.

I know my students learned to play my game. In fact, I know they were finishing assignments in the hallways right before class. They were leaning against lockers to get those last sentences on the page. How do I know that? Lots of times the writing would be slanted down the page! Somehow I don't think they were focusing on content at that point.

Somewhere inside of me, I knew this couldn't be all there was to it. Something was missing. I just couldn't get excited about teaching writing to my students—and of course, if I wasn't excited about *teaching* writing, my students weren't going to be excited about *learning* writing. I couldn't figure it out. I was such an avid reader, sharing my favorite books with my students. But you know what never occurred to me at the time? It was only later that I figured it out: I never wanted to share a piece of writing just because it used commas really well! And I bet that's true for you, too.

Then when I was an assistant principal in the 1980s (okay, maybe that was before you were born!), I had the privilege of learning of the work of Donald Graves and others who wrote about the writing process that many "real writers" use when they write. All the assistant principals in my district took part in intensive summer training to learn that process so we could help teachers with the challenge of teaching writing.

Things did improve greatly for teachers, students, *and* me after that. I still struggled, though, when I tried to come up with specific language to use in giving feedback to students. Once I wrote on a student's paper, "Keep working hard! You're almost there!" He asked me where he almost was! Clearly, my attempt at specific feedback didn't help that student very much. I still needed to find a better approach.

Then I learned from Vicki Spandel, Ruth Culham, and others about the traits of good writing and about the use of analytical or trait-based assessment. I learned about the importance of specific feedback from Robert Marzano. Suddenly I had the biggest revelation: I was teaching *writers*, not writing!

I realized that what I needed to do was jump right in there; the teachers, the students, and I would become writers together. Instead of just *describing* the process to teachers and students, I began actually *writing alongside them*. Together we practiced incorporating the traits of good writing, as well as assessing writing for each trait.

You know what happened? We all started to look forward to our writing time. Together we began to share and discuss our writing. Together we learned to assess and revise what we'd written. Together we became a community of readers and writers. It was so exciting!

I now invite you to join our community of readers and writers. Just turn the page and we'll begin our journey together.

Talking the Language of the Traits

In order for you to teach the traits of good writing, you and your students must understand what those traits are and recognize them when you see them. So the first of the six ways to teach the traits to your students is to talk the language of the traits, introducing and reinforcing trait terminology.

Who has to start that process? You do! In your classroom you are the CEO: Chief Example for Others. You are the learning leader, the role model. If it's going to happen, you're the one who's going to *make* it happen.

Does that sound overwhelming? Don't worry if you're not an expert on this already. Even if you're not at all familiar with the traits of good writing, that's okay. This chapter can serve as an overview for you as well.

Let me suggest to you one way you might consider introducing the traits to your students so that everyone can understand and recognize all six of them.

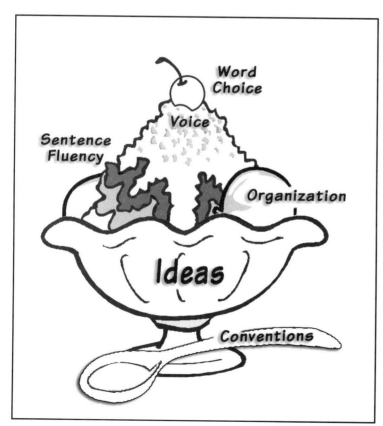

I like to use the metaphor of an ice cream sundae to introduce the traits of good writing. (For some reason, my mind always goes to food—especially anything with ice cream!) It's a simple idea that helps students to begin talking the language of the traits and thinking in terms of the six traits whenever they're involved in writing.

On page 85 you'll find a reproducible of an ice cream sundae. If you like, you can make an enlarged copy of that reproducible and post it in the classroom so you can refer to it as you introduce the traits. You might want to give a copy to each student, too. Hey, you might even want to celebrate with a real ice cream sundae party for your students after all the traits have been introduced. (I'll always figure out a way to get the eating in!)

Okay, here we go. As you introduce the traits to your students, keep in mind the reasons you're talking the trait language: you want your students to be able to recognize the traits, "talk the traits," and, we hope, infuse the traits of good writing into their own writing. At the end of each trait description, I've included a few key points about that trait. Those are the points you want your students to remember if they remember nothing else!

THE TRAIT OF IDEAS

The Sundae Bowl

The sundae bowl represents the trait of ideas. Just as the bowl is the starting point for making the sundae—the bowl holds the ice cream—the trait of ideas is the starting point for writing. The trait of ideas starts with a topic for writing. But there is much more to this trait than just a topic. Every topic needs to be a manageable size.

For Example

I remember talking once with a third grader who told me he was going to write his one-page report on all summer sports. One of the things I needed to do was meet with the student and help him narrow the topic of summer sports to something more manageable for one page. He decided he would write about floating down the Guadalupe River in Texas on an inner tube. Now *that* was a topic that was a more appropriate size!

Why is it important for the topic to be a manageable size? The real key to the trait of ideas is to focus on the specific details in a piece of writing. If you turn to page 86, you'll find a reproducible for a magnifying glass. That's exactly what you want your students to pretend they have when they're considering the trait of ideas.

Clear message
Focused topic
Specific details
What is the purpose?
Who is the audience?

The magnifying glass reminds each student that once she has her idea or topic, and once she's narrowed or focused that topic, then she needs to select quality details that are clear, specific, and appropriate for the audience and purpose of the writing. You might even want to run off copies of the reproducible on cardstock, cut them out, laminate them, and give one to each of your students.

The magnifying glass reinforces the importance of giving the reader unusual or interesting pieces of information. Emphasize to students that no one will really know how messy the closet is until they can "smell" the wet jogging shoes and socks or "see" the piles of dirty clothes shoved into the corner.

Teach your students that when they think of the trait of ideas, they should associate it with three things:

- Clear message
- Focused topic
- Specific details

THE TRAIT OF ORGANIZATION

The Scoops of Ice Cream

Tell your students to think of the scoops of ice cream as the trait of organization. For a sundae, it's good to have three scoops of ice cream: a scoop of vanilla, then a scoop of chocolate, and then another scoop of vanilla on the very top. (Are you like me and feeling just a little hungry right now? Oh, let's go ahead. I think we should make this sundae right now so we'll have the visual in front of us as we go through this!)

Alternating flavors in the three scoops of ice cream gives a pattern to the sundae. Tell your students that the trait of organization is the pattern of the writing. When you make a sundae, you always need a plan that includes who will eat your sundae, how you'll make it, and why you're making it. Writing always needs a plan, too. The plan considers who the audience will be (who will be reading the writing), the purpose of the writing, and what form it will take. Explain to students that just as each scoop of the sundae has a name (vanilla or chocolate), each part of the writing has a name.

The very first scoop of vanilla is the lead scoop. That scoop invites the eater to want more. The lead in writing is the first part of the writing that invites the reader to want more. Explain to students that when you eat a scoop of ice cream, it's not always that very first bite that makes you want more. Sometimes you have to take a few bites before you figure out you really want the whole thing. (Well, okay, maybe I'm stretching the point here, but you get the idea.) In the same way, a good lead in writing may not be the "first bite" or first sentence. Sometimes the reader has to read more to get hooked.

The chocolate scoop represents the middle of the sundae. In writing, the middle part needs to be easy to follow and understand. Good writers make sure they link their ideas and paragraphs together with appropriate transitions so the reader can follow the writing and understand it.

That final scoop of vanilla represents the conclusion in a piece of writing. Just as a sundae maker starts the sundae with a scoop of vanilla and ends with a scoop of vanilla, a good writer makes sure his conclusion relates back to the lead in some way. An effective conclusion tends to leave the writer with something to think about. I don't know about you, but I can do plenty of thinking about a good ice cream sundae!

Here are the key phrases you want your students to associate with the trait of organization:

- Lead: grab attention
- Transitions: logical and linking
- Conclusion: tie it together

THE TRAIT OF VOICE

All Those Mix-Ins

Is this the most fun part of making the sundae or what? Wow! You get to choose from all sorts of stuff to add to your sundae: sprinkles, nuts, candy bits, cookie pieces, and just about anything else you want. You get to make your sundae truly "you"!

Tell your students that is just what the trait of voice means in writing. If you're the author, then voice is "you" on the page: your personality, your enthusiasm, and your own individuality.

When you finish adding all the toppings to your sundae, you feel excited and happy. In writing, voice engages the reader and makes him feel something. That "something" can be happiness or sadness or some other feeling. Just as a sundae that's beautifully decorated with those toppings is begging to be eaten, writing with a strong voice is begging to be read or shared with others.

Teach your students that voice involves:

- Enthusiasm
- Involvement
- Feelings

THE TRAIT OF WORD CHOICE

The Just-Right Toppings

No sundae would be complete without those just-right toppings. My personal favorites are whipped cream (*real* whipped cream) and a cherry. Choosing just the right words to convey the author's meaning—often words that create pictures in the reader's mind—is what we mean by the trait of word choice. We all know that too much whipped cream on a sundae can make you heavy. In the same way, when students use too many adjectives and adverbs, their writing seems heavy. Good writers go for precise nouns and lively verbs without overdoing the use of adjectives and adverbs.

Are you ready for the next list? Here are the key phrases you want students to associate with word choice:

- Words as pictures
- Precise nouns
- Lively verbs

THE TRAIT OF SENTENCE FLUENCY

The Syrups

It's so much fun to choose a flavor or two of syrup and add that to the sundae. The syrups flow down the ice cream. In writing, the trait of sentence fluency means the writing flows smoothly and easily. One sentence seems to glide into the next, lots of times with a real rhythm. Often the writer reads the writing aloud to hear how it sounds. Is it easy to read aloud? Are the sentence beginnings varied? Are there different numbers of words in each sentence? The trait of sentence fluency is a trait you can hear.

Teach your students to remember that sentence fluency involves:

- Flow and rhythm
- Different sentence beginnings
- Different sentence lengths

THE TRAIT OF CONVENTIONS

The Spoon

The last thing you do before you start to eat your sundae is pick up your spoon. In writing, the trait you want to pay attention to at the very end is the trait of conventions. When I was growing up and then in my early years as a teacher, I picked up the spoon first. In other words, I focused almost totally on the trait of conventions: the capitalization, the usage, the punctuation, the spelling, the paragraphing, and the overall neatness of the handwriting.

Now I know that the trait of conventions is one of the *last* things many good writers consider; they understand how important it is to get their ideas down on paper first, in a way that's organized and fluent, includes good word choices, and incorporates the writer's unique voice. (Besides, if you focus on conventions first and then decide to work on word choice, you have to go back and check conventions all over again.) Spelling, punctuation, and all the rest still matter; you just want to save them for last. So here we go with the last list of key phrases. When you think of the trait of conventions, remember:

- Edit for CAPS (capitalization, agreement and usage, punctuation, spelling)
- Check the presentation

PUTTING IT ALL TOGETHER

The Whole Sundae

Wow! The sundae is complete! Turn to the "Key Words & Phrases" reproducible on page 87 to help your students remember the traits of good writing. You might want to make a poster of this reproducible for your classroom and/or give a copy to each student.

I know what you're probably thinking now. Do I introduce these traits all at once? How long do I spend on each trait? How does this enhance the writing instruction in my classroom? Settle down, or as we say here in Texas: "Don't get your panties in a wad!" We will address all of these issues in later chapters. For now, you've learned the first of six ways to teach the traits of good writing to your students: talking the language of the traits. Use the ice cream sundae metaphor if you want to as a way to introduce the traits to your students.

Now let's continue on our journey and look at some wonderful pieces of literature you can use to teach the traits.

Read, Read, Read

The second way to teach the traits of good writing to your students is with literature. When you read aloud to your students, you're providing them with great models of how good writers incorporate the six basic traits in their work. When your students hear a good story, they hear the language of good writers and they become better equipped to then use those traits in their own writing. Besides, if you read aloud to your students, you greatly enrich the writing instruction in your classroom.

Sometimes a teacher will say to me, "I just don't have enough time to read aloud to my students anymore. My days are so packed as it is." I know how packed every school day is. I really do. But keep in mind that you don't have to read for a long time each day. Just 5–10 minutes of reading aloud can make a big difference for your students, reinforcing how good writers create good work and providing models for the students to follow.

You probably have some favorite chapter books that you enjoy reading aloud with your students already. But don't stop there! When you read aloud, try to include all kinds of text: newspaper stories; magazine articles; informational text, such as travel brochures or CD liner notes; children's trade books; or descriptions of items listed on restaurant menus. One of my favorites is a description of a hot fudge cake that I found on a menu. (Can you tell I love sweets?) Show your students that the traits of good writing are found everywhere because good writing is found everywhere!

This chapter lists more than 50 children's books that you can use as models of the six traits of good writing. I've noted why I've included each book. But that doesn't mean you need to limit yourself to just the books on this list. Nor does it mean that you have to use the books in exactly the ways I've described. You might want to add others, use some of these listed under one trait to illustrate another trait, or substitute different books entirely. Go for it!

I don't want you to think that you have to skip this important part of teaching the traits because you don't have these particular titles. Believe me, once you learn the traits, you can go to your school library, the public library, or your favorite bookstore, pick out virtually any children's book, and find in it at least some of the traits you want to illustrate to your students. And do you know the best part? Once your students learn the traits, they'll be able to tell you what trait jumps out at *them* from a particular book and why.

A Quick Tip

A few of the books I've included here may be out of print. I've included them anyway because I feel they're well worth a visit to the school or local library. Also, I've had really good luck finding these books in the used-book sections of Amazon.com. Sometimes you just need to be a little resourceful!

THE TRAIT OF IDEAS

Books to Use as Examples

These particular books really illustrate the critical attributes of the trait of ideas. You remember those attributes, right? The ones you stressed to your students? That's right: clear message, focused topic, and specific details. Here are some titles that demonstrate those concepts especially well.

- *Zoom,* by Istvan Banyai
- *Re-Zoom,* by Istvan Banyai
  Each of these two wordless picture books re-creates the effect of a camera lens that is gradually expanding its focus—sometimes with unexpected results. Read the books backwards to give students an example of zooming in on just the right details in a piece of writing.

- *Big Moon Tortilla,* by Joy Cowley
  When a young girl has a problem, her grandmother consoles her with timeless advice, based on old Native American wisdom. The language is tremendously evocative; you'd see pictures in your head even if the wonderful illustrations weren't there.

- *I Heard a Bluebird Sing*, *edited by Bernice E. Cullen*
  Students from around the country selected their favorite poems by Aileen Fisher, winner of the National Council of Teachers of English Award for Poetry for Children, and those 41 selections are the basis of this anthology. Use these beloved poems to show students strong figurative language as well as clear ideas. On page nine, the author offers her thoughts on writing; be sure to share those ideas with your students.

- *Mrs. Piccolo's Easy Chair*, *by Jean Jackson*
  This is the story of a huge chair that acts like a person. With its owner, Mrs. Piccolo, the chair even goes along to the grocery store, swallowing up in its great purple cushions anyone who gets in the way of its quest for cheese puffs! Through illustrations, lots of detail, and plenty of silliness, the book is sure to delight the reader.

- *Guts,* *by Gary Paulsen*
  In this autobiographical book, Gary Paulsen reveals the real-life incidents that inspired the Brian Robeson character in *Hatchet* and other Paulsen novels. It's a great book for showing students one way authors get ideas from real life.

- *Rotten Teeth,* *by Laura Simms*
  This book, filled with specific details, is another one based on the author's real-life experiences. The main character, Melissa Hermann, has nothing to take to her first-grade classroom for show-and-tell until she gets an idea. She decides to take a jar of rotten teeth from her father's dental office, which is in the back of her house. She goes to school with the jar of teeth and proceeds to take a tooth from the jar to give to each student. Her teacher is not amused!

- *Through the Cracks,* *by Carolyn Sollman*
  The trait of ideas is especially evident here as both the words and the illustrations address a timely educational issue: all students need to find meaning, challenge, and relevance in school. When the children in this story fail to find that meaning, they shrink and literally fall between the cracks—gradually returning to normal size only when they discover

classrooms in which students are engaged and their excitement for learning reignited.

- ***Alexander and the Terrible, Horrible, No Good, Very Bad Day,*** *by Judith Viorst*

  Everyone has a bad day sometimes. Read this favorite aloud to your students and then challenge each student to use the main idea of the book as the basis for writing her own bad-day story.

- ***Carl's Birthday,*** *by Alexandra Day*
- ***Pancakes for Breakfast,*** *by Tomie dePaola*

  Wordless picture books, including these two engaging examples, can provide wonderful stimuli for student writing. Ask your students to take inspiration from the illustrations and provide their own words to create stories.

- ***The Mysteries of Harris Burdick,*** *by Chris Van Allsburg*

  Here is a collection of beautiful and mysterious illustrations, each accompanied by a very short, but enticing, description sure to fire students' imaginations. Invite each student to choose one of the pictures and invent his own story to go with it.

THE TRAIT OF ORGANIZATION

Books to Use as Examples

Look at these titles for examples of great leads, smooth transitions, and effective conclusions.

- ***No More Dead Dogs,*** *by Gordon Korman*

  This is a delightful and entertaining story of an eighth-grade football player, Wallace Wallace, who gets sent to detention for expressing his true views of his teacher's favorite book. Use this as an example of a lead that doesn't appear in the first sentence. You have to read a few pages in to be truly hooked!

- *Animals Nobody Loves*, by Seymour Simon

  Through 20 photos and accompanying text, Seymour Simon reveals information about some misunderstood animals. The text for each illustration really has no lead, so the book works well as a basis for letting students practice writing different kinds of leads of their own.

- *Book! Book! Book!,* by Deborah Bruss

  This is a delightful story of a group of animals that want books but have a hard time explaining this to the librarian. The author uses a simple organizational pattern that's worth pointing out to your students. Besides, it doesn't hurt to share with students a book that suggests that even animals want to read.

- *Fireboat: The Heroic Adventures of the John J. Harvey*, by Maira Kalman

  The *John J. Harvey*, built in 1931, played a heroic role on September 11, 2001. This story uses transitions in a very clever way: dates associated with the history of the boat help the reader move along through the text.

- *Walter the Farting Dog*, by William Kotzwinkle and Glenn Murray

  Walter, who turns out to be the hero when his famous flatulence scares away some burglars, will be a hit with your students. The transitions in this tale are effective but not so obvious that they take away from the story; discuss with students what makes them work. This book is also a great model for the trait of sentence fluency. It's a joy to read aloud with a kind of singsong rhythm.

- *Dog Breath: The Horrible Trouble with Hally Tosis*, by Dav Pilkey

  This is a humorous picture book about a special dog with horrible breath. It has great transitions, and you can use it to demonstrate word choice as well.

- *When I Was Young in the Mountains*, by Cynthia Rylant

  Most students are used to reading books that are organized chronologically, but it's important to show your students other organizational patterns, too, and to discuss those patterns together.

This book relates childhood memories without using a chronological structure.

- ***On Call Back Mountain***, *by Eve Bunting*
  The fun and affection inherent in the relationship between two brothers and an elderly man are movingly described in this picture book. It's a good example of a circular conclusion—one that echoes the beginning. And because the wording is almost lyrical, it's a great selection to demonstrate word choice and sentence fluency as well.

- ***The Greedy Triangle***, *by Marilyn Burns*
  Through its main character, a triangle, this book introduces children to geometry. It gives another example of a circular conclusion.

- ***But I Waannt It!***, *by Dr. Laura Schlessinger*
  Here's a good example of a strong conclusion, as the main character reflects on what's happened and gains new insight into what it is that really makes him happy.

THE TRAIT OF VOICE

Books to Use as Examples

The following books demonstrate outstanding use of voice. They show enthusiasm and involvement, and they do a great job of bringing out the reader's feelings.

- ***Woman Hollering Creek***, *by Sandra Cisneros*
  Sandra Cisneros's voice comes through in each of the short stories in this collection, creating a series of unforgettable characters. One of the stories, "Eleven," is particularly delightful.

- ***Don't Read This Book, Whatever You Do!***, *by Kalli Dakos*
  This is a collection of 37 poems, all full of voice and all related to things that could happen only in a classroom. It's a great collection that will entertain both your students and you.

- *Rainbows, Head Lice, and Pea-Green Tile*, *by Brod Bagert*
  Discussing everything from the troublemaker with perfect attendance to parents who take over their children's school projects, these poems are actually for *you*. They will make you laugh and cry as you read some of the many voices of teachers!

- *Because of Winn-Dixie*, *by Kate DiCamillo*
  From the very first page, your students will be absolutely enchanted by Kate DiCamillo's voice. When you look at all the awards this story has received, it's clear that plenty of others respond to her just as strongly.

- *Uncovered!*, *by Paul Jennings*
  If you want to delight your students, read them this collection of funny, weird, and wacky stories. Jennings's voice comes through clearly in each one. A particular favorite of mine is "A Mouthful," about a father's insistence on playing practical jokes until his embarrassed daughter finally gives him a dose of his own medicine.

- *The Dot and the Line*, *by Norton Juster*
  Using both humor and voice extremely well, this book tells the story of a straight line in love with a red dot. It's a wonderful love story that manages to teach math concepts along the way.

- *The Big Wide-Mouthed Frog*, *by Keith Faulkner*
  This is a delightful, voice-filled retelling of an old American tale—the story of a frog who brags to everyone and then learns it's sometimes better to keep your mouth shut!

- *Guys Write for Guys Read*, *edited by Jon Scieszka*
  Yes, that really is the title! This is a collection of 92 stories, memoirs, bits of advice, poems, comics, and drawings from a wide variety of contributors, each piece selected especially for its appeal to young male readers. In part because each person's voice comes through in his own contribution, this anthology offers a good way to encourage more boys to read.

- ***The True Story of the Three Little Pigs**, by Jon Scieszka*
  Readers delight in the voice in this book because the story is told from the wolf's point of view.

- ***Kevin and His Dad**, by Irene Smalls*
  This is the story of a young boy and his dad and the day they spend together. The writer's evident feelings of excitement, pride, and pleasure evoke similar emotions in the reader—a sure sign of strong voice.

- ***Faithful Elephants**, by Yukio Tsuchiya*
  During World War II, when Tokyo was under air attack, the Japanese worried about the possibility of bombs falling on the Tokyo zoo. They were afraid that if the zoo were bombed, the animals might run loose and kill the local people, so they decided to kill the animals—but killing the magnificent elephants wasn't easy. It's hard to read this book, which inspires a heightened sensitivity to the plight of the elephants, without feeling a deep sense of sadness.

THE TRAIT OF WORD CHOICE

Books to Use as Examples

These books are full of precise nouns, lively verbs, and words that create pictures in the reader's mind.

- ***A Cold Snap!**, by Audrey B. Baird*
  This is a collection of 22 poems that, through the author's clever choice of words, create the sense that autumn has arrived and winter is approaching fast.

- ***More Than Anything Else**, by Marie Bradby*
  Not only does this fictional story of the life of Booker T. Washington give readers lots of imagery and great examples of the trait of word choice, it also demonstrates to students how important literacy is in their lives. More than anything else, a young Booker T. Washington wants to learn to read.

- *A Mink, a Fink, a Skating Rink: What Is a Noun?*
- *Dearly, Nearly, Insincerely: What Is an Adverb?*
- *Hairy, Scary, Ordinary: What Is an Adjective?*
- *To Root, to Toot, to Parachute: What Is a Verb?*
- *Under, Over, By the Clover: What Is a Preposition?*

  This series of playful rhyming books by Brian P. Cleary, each focusing on a different part of speech, provides the reader with wonderfully memorable lines such as, "Adverbs will frequently end in 'L-Y,' as in viciously, ultra-suspiciously sly." They offer great ways to help students remember how to distinguish adverbs, adjectives, and all the rest.

- *Donavan's Word Jar, by Monalisa DeGross*

  Here's a way to show your students the power of words and, perhaps, spark interest in starting a class word jar. The main character, Donavan, loves to collect words. When his word jar fills up, his grandma helps him figure out what to do.

- *Miss Alaineus: A Vocabulary Disaster, by Debra Frasier*

  Your students will enjoy the playful use of language in this book. They'll also appreciate the story of Sage, the main character, who gets really confused about a vocabulary word. The vocabulary parade at the end of the story can be the basis for a great classroom strategy.

- *A Chocolate Moose for Dinner, by Fred Gwynne*

  This book contains a series of delightful examples of figurative and playful language. Use them as a source of patterns for students to use in creating and illustrating their own writing.

- *Kites Sail High: A Book About Verbs*
- *Merry-Go-Round: A Book About Nouns*
- *A Cache of Jewels and Other Collective Nouns*

  All of these Ruth Heller books are filled with delightful vocabulary and great illustrations. Use them to teach parts of speech.

- ***Gullywasher Gulch**, by Marianne Mitchell*

  You'll find lots of playful language in the tale of Ebenezer Overall, who treasures his collection of "useless junk" almost as much as the gold nuggets he's saving for a rainy, "gullywasher" day.

- ***Sir Cumference and the First Round Table: A Math Adventure**, by Cindy Neuschwander*

  The author uses words in a very clever way to introduce readers to the language of mathematics.

THE TRAIT OF SENTENCE FLUENCY

Books to Use as Examples

Each of these titles is a joy to read aloud.

- ***The Important Book**, by Margaret Wise Brown*

  Describing "the important thing about" a spoon, rain, a shoe, and more, this is a great book to read aloud to demonstrate the trait of sentence fluency. It's also perfect for inspiring students to add their own pages, expanding on the "important" theme.

- ***Girls A to Z**, by Eve Bunting*

  Eve Bunting's playful, rhyming text invites girls to go for their dreams.

- ***Click, Clack, Moo***
- ***Giggle, Giggle, Quack***

  These Doreen Cronin stories are entertaining and a pleasure to read aloud, making them wonderful examples of the trait of sentence fluency. Your students will delight at the adventures of Farmer Brown and his animals.

- ***Giraffes Can't Dance**, by Giles Andreae*

  Full of rhyme and rhythm, this is a tale of how a giraffe's dream comes true because someone believes in him.

- *My Little Sister Ate One Hare*, by Bill Grossman

  The little sister ate not only one hare, but also lots of other creepy things. This is a great read-aloud. It's also a good jumping-off point. Let students use it as inspiration for writing additional pages on the same subject.

- *Winnie the Witch*, by Korky Paul and Valerie Thomas

  This story of Winnie the Witch and her black cat, Wilbur, has a rhythm and flow that make it a pleasure to read aloud.

- *Spaghetti Eddie*, by Ryan SanAngelo

  This story of Eddie and his spaghetti has a good, zippy tempo that makes this a great example of the trait of sentence fluency.

- *CDC?*, by William Steig

  This collection of word puzzles—I call them "license-plate writing"—must be read aloud to be figured out! After they read it, have students create their own word puzzles.

THE TRAIT OF CONVENTIONS

Books to Use as Examples

Books that illustrate the trait of conventions sound like they'd be about as exciting to read as the dictionary. But don't underestimate the dictionary!

- *Punctuation Takes a Vacation*, by Robin Pulver

  This lighthearted story, which includes things like postcard notes sent home by vacationing punctuation marks, shows students how much punctuation is needed in writing.

- *How to Spell It*, by Harriet Wittels and Joan Greisman

  Students will turn to this before a dictionary because it has only one rule: red is right. The student looks up a word the way he thinks it's spelled. If that spelling's in red, the student is right. If it's in black, he's incorrect, and he'll find the correct spelling in red beside the misspelled version.

3

Invitations to Write

This chapter is all about giving your students a wide variety of writing experiences. Now I'm not talking about the writing they'll do during a more formal block of writing time in your classroom. I'm not talking about activities that necessarily focus on one of the traits at a time. I'm talking about writing you'll invite them to do all day long, whenever they can. I'm talking about "real-world" writing.

The writing experiences don't need to be long or sophisticated or presented perfectly. After all, think of the writing that you've done this week. I bet you haven't written a five-paragraph essay! Maybe you've written a grocery list, a note to a student or parent, an e-mail message, and a "things-to-do" list. That's real-world writing. Answering questions at the end of a textbook chapter is not! Students need to know how to write *in ways they can use in the real world.*

To reach that goal, it's important for your students to know that in their classroom there is always some writing they can do—not busywork but writing that's meaningful, and often quite fun and creative as well. You need to set up the expectation that when students are finished with a particular assignment, waiting for a conference with you, or waiting for the bell to ring, they should be engaged in some kind of writing.

You're probably doing a pretty good job of this in reading. I bet you have a reading corner in your room filled with lots of reading material for your students. What I'm suggesting is that you create a classroom *writing* area as well, and that you fill it with materials and ideas to encourage all sorts of writing. You and I will get to the more structured writing in a later chapter. For now, we're focusing on letting students know that we *value* writing—all kinds of writing. After all, when your students are involved with writing of any kind, they're engaged with the traits of good writing.

I bet you're thinking, "Where in my classroom will all this writing take place?" I bet you've also guessed my answer: Your class needs a spot that's dedicated to writing. Call it the "Writing Café" (there I go again, thinking about food) or "Writing Corner" or whatever you want, but you need to have a place designated for writing. A designated place sends the message that writing is important in your classroom.

If you can, set up your writing area so that it includes a computer and a bulletin board. Students can use the computer for writing and then you can post that writing on the bulletin board. If you have a couple of extra desks or a table, those can be a part of the writing area, too.

The writing area needs to be well stocked with all sorts of things for students to write on (plain paper, colored paper, index cards, and spiral notebooks) and things to write with (pencils and erasers, pens, markers, and gel pens), as well as the tools writers use (dictionaries, thesauruses, staplers, scissors, hole punch, folders, and so on). Include plenty of magazines and catalogs, too. Stackable trays make nice storage bins. You might want to provide students with their own pocket folders, too, so each student can keep a folder in the writing area with some of his writing in it.

A Quick Tip

Take a picture of the way the writing area is supposed to look when it's all cleaned up. Post the picture next to the writing area and tell students that when they leave the area, it should look just like the picture.

Once you have the writing area set up, students need to know how they will be held accountable for writing done there. If you use writing folders, you might collect them periodically for spot checks, or you might post schedules so your students know when you'll be looking at their folders. You might also designate a time at the end of each week when students share with the class some of the things they've worked on in the writing area.

Of course, the writing area isn't meant to take the place of specific instruction in the traits of good writing or the more formal classroom time that you spend writing with your students. Rather, the writing area *extends* writing time in your classroom by making sure students always have an opportunity to be writing when they have a few minutes of free time.

Now, are you ready for more than 20 meaningful and fun writing activities for your writing area? Well, let's get going. Just remember to explicitly model each of the following activities for your students. If you're not sure where to find an appropriate model, I'd suggest you use your own writing. The students can learn so much from seeing you write in front of them!

ALL SIX TRAITS

Class Newsletter

Students publish class newsletters that are sent home once a week to the parents. When I was a building principal, many of the teachers had their students do this. Each newsletter was only one page, created on the computer. It would include announcements of any special events for the week, birthdays, and information about units of study.

Students took turns filling various "contributing editor" roles—reporting what was being studied during the week, giving opinions about things going on in school, and so on. By Friday each week, the newsletter had to be complete and printed so it could be sent home the following Monday. In addition to extending writing time, this was a great chance for students to take responsibility for the learning in the classroom. And it didn't hurt in terms of building relationships with parents either.

"Show Me" Books

Many times you probably ask your students to *show* the reader something rather than just telling something. Specific details, great word choice, and images help a reader "see" what the writer's describing. To help students develop that aspect of their writing, post a different "Show Me" prompt for students each week.

On a sentence strip, write a word or phrase such as "a rainy day," then challenge students to "show" that concept in no more than 30 words. Create a class "Show Me" book of the student writing that comes from these prompts.

Possible "Show Me" Prompts

- a jack-o-lantern
- a snowman
- a toddler
- a doctor's office
- a forest
- a kite

All About Me

Use the reproducible on page 88 as a springboard to encourage students to write about themselves. Notice that the questions are keyed to the levels of thinking in Bloom's Taxonomy. If you like, compile the responses into a class "All About Us" book.

Name Chants

Students use the first letters of their first and last names to write a chant that describes them. Suzy Jones, for example, might say, "Suzy Jones, Sensational Juggler." Keep this writing going by having students do the same thing for their family members, friends, pets, and so on.

License-Plate Writing

Students create "license plates" that play with language. An example might be CAND4U or "Candy for You." (For inspiration, show students William Steig's book *CDC?*.) Identify an area such as a bulletin board in the classroom and invite students to post their "license plates" there. Ask the other students to try to guess the meanings.

Graffiti Board

Cover a wall with bulletin-board paper and have plenty of markers and pens available. Invite students to go to the "Graffiti Board" and write their comments about books they've read. To keep this writing activity going, let other students respond, in writing, on the same board. There's just something fun about writing on the wall!

CHARACTER-TAC-TOE

After reading a book and picking a character, choose three activities in the tic-tac-toe design. The three activities need to make a row horizontally, vertically, or diagonally. You may decide three activities are enough, or you may decide to keep going and complete more activities. You may work with one or more partners on one of the activities.

1 Write about a day in the life of your character.	2 Create a collage that tells something about your character.	3 Create a rap or song to describe your character.
4 Create a timeline of the important events in your character's life.	5 FREE SPACE (your choice)	6 With a group of three other students, write a fairy tale that includes your character.
7 Write a biography of your character.	8 Write about how your character would react to winning the lottery.	9 Write a poem that reveals your character's strengths and weaknesses.

I have chosen ___Deltora Quest___ (character)

from ___The Lake of Tears___ (book)

I have chosen to complete these activities: # _1_ , # _5_ , and # _9_ .

Student Signature: _Christopher Wilkes_ Date: _April 4, 2006_

Teacher Signature: _Jane Jones_ Date: _April 4, 2006_

Character-Tac-Toe

Start with the reproducible on page 89 and make a copy for each student. Explain that each student is to choose a character from a book he's been reading and then select from the grid three assignments he's going to complete; the selections have to form a tic-tac-toe pattern (making a row either horizontally, vertically, or diagonally). The student then completes the assignments chosen on the "Character-Tac-Toe."

Wordless Picture Books

Remember how I told you earlier that wordless picture books are great for getting students to create their own stories? Here's their chance! The pictures are there; it's just the words that are missing.

Writing Bingo

Consider using the "Writing Bingo" reproducible on page 90. Challenge your students to complete a "Writing Bingo" during a grading period by choosing one column from the reproducible and completing all of the writing activities in that column.

WRITING BINGO

Thank You Note	Wise Sayings	Poem	Fable	Movie Review
Recipe	Rhymes	Folk Tale	Bumper Sticker	Dream
Directions from One Place to Another	Memories	FREE SPACE (your choice)	Comic Strip	Lead
Rules for a Game	Dialogue	TV Commercial	Greeting Card	Conclusion
Wonderful Words	Puns	Opinion	Grocery List	Mystery

A Big List of Lists

Post in the writing area a list of lists your students could make. They could make lists of foods, movies, TV shows, colors, friends, things to do on the weekend, things that are round, things that are square, one-syllable words, two-syllable words, books, animals—you get the idea. But don't stop there. After students create lists and put them in their writing folders, ask each student to write a story with her list, to make a word search or crossword puzzle from the list, or to put the list in alphabetical order.

Magazine & Calendar Pictures

Keep a stack of magazine and calendar pictures in your writing center; they're great starters for any kind of writing. For example, you might have your students take a calendar picture of a group of people and write a dialogue between the people without using the word "said."

100 T.H.I.N.K. Questions

Start with the "100 T.H.I.N.K. Questions" reproducibles on pages 91–94, roughly 50–100 slips of paper, and five paper lunch bags. Label each bag with one of the letters in the word THINK. Write a question from one of the reproducibles on each slip of paper, and then drop the paper into the appropriate paper bag. Invite each student to pull a question from one of the bags and respond to it in writing. He should then staple the question to his written answer and place both in his writing folder. Plan a specific time each week when students can share their answers.

Voice Sticks

Start with a batch of craft sticks; on each one, write a prompt or beginning thought for student writing. A thought might be, "Hooray, hooray . . . ," "If I could pick a pet . . . ," "If I were the principal . . . ," or "A special gift I received . . . ." Place all of the "Voice Sticks" in an old soup can, and then invite each student to draw a stick out of the can and respond to or continue the thought on a piece of paper.

Ideas for Voice Sticks

- If I were the teacher I would . . .

- If I could give one piece of advice to any person in history, that advice would be . . .

- Describe a dream you had recently. Provide as many details as possible.

- The best lesson my grandparent (parent) ever taught me was . . .

- In 20 years I will be . . .

- Tell about an event in your life that caused a change in you.

- I was most angry when . . .

- I was happiest when . . .

- My worst mistake was . . .

- My best accomplishment was . . .

- If you and your best friend could have a free limousine for 24 hours, where would you go and what would you do?

- You have the freedom to travel to any city or country in the world. Where would you go and why?

- What would you do if you were president of the United States?

- You have $100,000 to give away. You cannot spend it on yourself. What would you do with the money?

- The qualities that make a best friend are . . .

- If you were an insect, what kind would you be and why?

Who Can't Play?

This is a simple writing activity that will get your students thinking at higher levels. Have students brainstorm lists of about five words, then ask them to cross out the word that doesn't belong and label the rest of the words. (See the "Who Can't Play?" reproducible on page 95 for some lists of words to get you started.) The higher-level thinking comes in when they have to figure out the labels. You'll be surprised at what they come up with.

For example, let's say I list five words:

- One
- Six
- Ten
- Banana
- Seven

Which one would you say can't play? Yes, "banana," because the rest are numbers. The label would be numbers.

But what if I gave you this list?

- Policeman
- Doctor
- Teacher
- Counselor
- Plumber

You might say "plumber" can't play because the rest of those professions work with people. I say "teacher" can't play because the rest of those professions make money! See? It's all in how you label it.

Wanted Posters for Vocabulary Words

Have your students use their vocabulary words to create Wanted posters and then hang the posters in the classroom. To begin, give students large sheets of paper and lots of markers. The word goes at the top of each sheet. The student draws a picture to show the word. Then, underneath the picture, the student fills in four lines:

- Crime: (brief definition of the word)
- Alias: (different forms of the word)
- Last Seen With: (synonym for the word)
- Reward: (sentence using the word)

WANTED!!!

Erupt

Crime: to appear suddenly and violently

Alias: erupted, eruption, erupting, erupts

Last Seen With: emerge

Reward: The lava began to erupt from the volcano.

Biopoems

A biopoem, as you may know, is a type of poem in which the subject is the writer of the poem. Line 1 of the biopoem would be the first name of the student. The poem continues, using a format something like this one.

Line	Description	Example
1	First name of the author	Paul
2	Four adjectives to describe the author	Athletic, brave, considerate, gentle
3	Relatives of the author (list three or four)	Cousin Rachel, brother Brad, Aunt Martha
4	Lover of . . . (list three or four items, people)	Lover of pizza, baseball, ice cream, movies
5	Who feels (list three or four emotions)	Who feels excited, happy, confident
6	Who needs (list three or four items)	Who needs friends, family, TV, sports
7	Who fears (list three or four things)	Who fears snakes, striking out, oversleeping
8	Who gives (list three or four items)	Who gives more than 100%, lunch money, time to friends
9	Who would like to see (list three or four items)	Who would like to see the Astros win a World Series, Fenway Park, world peace
10	Resident of	Resident of Texas
11	Last name of the author	Marsh

Biopoems work really well for studying content, too. Just modify the format as needed. Maybe you want students to review material about your state that they've covered in social studies. You might modify the biopoem format and have them follow a list that includes the state flower, current governor, major cities, and so on.

Telephone Writing

Work with your class to set up a chart like the one shown in the illustration. The first column is for characters, the second column is for settings, the third is for problems, and the fourth is for solutions. Each is numbered from 0–9.

With your students, brainstorm a list of their favorite 10 characters, 10 story settings, 10 possible problems, and 10 possible solutions. After setting up the chart, laminate it and hang it on the wall in the writing area. Each student can use the last four digits of his phone number to write a unique story using the character that matches the first digit, the setting that matches the second digit, the problem that matches the third, and the solution that matches the fourth. To use the chart again, have each student base his story on a friend's phone number, a relative's number, or some other number he calls often. You'll be amazed at how creative these stories will be.

Telephone Writing

Characters	Settings	Problems	Solutions
0 Harry Potter	0 At school	0 Get in trouble	0 Tell a friend
1 Hank the Cowdog	1 In the park	1 Find money	1 Return a favor
2 Fudge	2 At the movies	2 Lose dog	2 Ask for help
3	3	3	3
4	4	4	4
5		5	5
			6

Morning Message

Each morning, have a different student write a morning message to all of her classmates and then read it aloud to the class. The message could include items such as lunch choices for the day, any special events, or birthdays.

Convince Me to Buy It!

In the writing area, provide pictures of clothing, games, etc. from catalogs. The assignment is for a student to choose an item and then use no more than 50 words to convince a classmate to buy that item. This encourages students to think carefully about the trait of word choice.

Word Detective

Take a stack of index cards, write a vocabulary word on each one, and put the cards in a box. Once a week, have each student choose a card and then "become" the word on that card. Then start asking questions. Use the ones listed below or make up your own. Explain that each student should answer as the word would answer, while the rest of the class tries to figure out which word the student has.

For Example

If a student had the word "computer," then he would take on that role as he answered the questions. His responses might be along these lines:

- Who are your relatives? "calculator, typewriter"
- Is there anything you don't like? "viruses and bugs"
- Are you useful? "I work very fast and accurately."
- Do you have any goals? "I want to be in every classroom and every home."

Daffy Dictionaries

Provide your students with lists of root words, prefixes, and suffixes, along with the meanings of all of those. Invite students to combine suffixes, roots, and prefixes to create daffy or imaginary words and definitions. At a later time, have them take turns letting other students guess the meanings they've assigned to their "words." For example, can you guess the meaning of my daffy dictionary word "phonesia"? My definition is "the act of dialing a phone number and forgetting whom you were calling just as the phone starts to ring."

Challenge Links

Start with the "Challenge Links" reproducible on pages 96–98. Run them off on colored paper and cut the strips apart. Challenge students to figure out the linking word for each pair and to fill in each of the lines. For example, for the words "boy" and "grab," the link is "bag," making "bagboy" and "grab bag." Once they've completed their links, students can fold and staple the links to create a chain and then put the chain on the bulletin board.

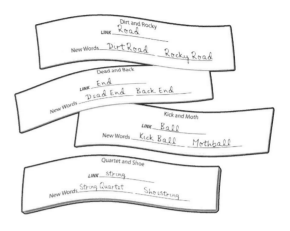

Class Word Book

Invite students to use spare moments to go to the writing area and add words to the class word book. All you have to do is create a page for each category of words and let the students do the rest.

For Example

Categories for pages in class word books can run the gamut. If you want to use every letter of the alphabet, you might take the following as a jumping-off point for your own inspiration:

- Amazing words
- Bewitching words
- Color words
- Dangerous words
- Everyday words
- Feeling words
- Gentle words
- Harsh words
- Icy words
- Joyful words
- Kind words
- Lively words
- Music words
- Night words
- Odd words
- Proud words
- Quaint words
- Rainy words
- Silly words
- Thirsty words
- Understanding words
- Vacation words
- Wonderful words
- Xerox words (words related to the copying process)
- Yard words
- Zany words

Practice Makes Permanent

One of the best things you can do for your students is to get in the habit of writing in front of them often and thinking aloud as you write. When you do that, you manage two things at once: you give students a model of what the writing process is really like, and you show them ways to incorporate the traits of good writing in their own work.

Recently I bought some new running shoes. (Actually, I don't run—I sort of jog—but I like to say that I run. I think it sounds better.) When I was in the store looking at all the shoes, I kept seeing the Nike boxes with their slogan: "Just Do It!" That slogan used to apply to writing in my classroom. I wanted my students to "Just Do It!"—just sit there and write. Now I'm convinced that a better way to think about writing in the classroom is this: "First *I* do it (modeling with your own writing). Then *we* do it (as you let students practice with you). *Then* they do it (as students apply what they've learned to their own writing)."

That's certainly a different twist. I used to avoid writing in front of my students at all costs. Pretty much the only time I would do it was when I was teaching some sort of grammar lesson or maybe using a graphic organizer to teach them some kind of formula for a particular kind of writing. I wouldn't have considered just "thinking out loud" and starting to write in front of them.

When all you do is write grammar stuff or formula stuff, you make writing detached and mechanical. Remember, you're teaching *writers*. You want them to take some risks with their writing. You need to take a risk yourself! Stand right beside your overhead, face your students, and write. They'll be more willing to try writing when they see you do it.

There's another reason why writing in front of students is a good thing: it lets them see how the process works. Let me explain.

Because I travel all over the place now working with teachers and administrators, I often have to rent a car late at night and drive to a location where I'll be working the next day. I'm not so good at night driving.

One night I was in Georgia, trying to find the school where I'd be working with teachers the next morning. It was late and it was dark and I was about as lost as it's possible to be. I found the school all right, but I got so confused trying to find my way out of the school parking lot that I ended up driving around on the high-school jogging track! How embarrassing!

I sometimes think that driving my rental car late at night is really like writing. (Have you noticed that I sometimes think just about *everything* is really like writing?) I can see only as far as the headlights on the car will allow, but I like to think I can make it all the way to my destination with just those headlights and maybe a good road map guiding me. (If only road maps included school parking lots!)

Writing is like that. In writing you don't have to know everything you'll pass along the way. You really just have to have a general sense of where you're going and then navigate one small section at a time. You'll gain writing confidence in front of your students, and your students will gain confidence, too, if you approach writing this way. You need to show them how it's done— with all the wrong turns and corrections that can involve!

In this chapter, you'll find lots of ideas for mini-lessons in writing. Every one of these mini-lessons involves explicit instruction in one of the six traits. Each can be completed in 10–15 minutes and will reinforce learning by giving students a chance to practice. Every one can have a powerful impact on student writing. And virtually every one of them involves your writing in front of your students.

The Parking Lot

Purpose: Sometimes a student will say, "I can't think of a thing to write about." Sound familiar? This lesson offers a visual way for students to "park" topics they can write about later.

Materials & Preparation: Starting with "The Parking Lot" reproducible on page 99, make an enlarged copy and turn it into a large poster for the classroom wall. Add plenty of Post-it notes for student use. In addition, make one copy of the reproducible for each student.

Model: Tell students that one of the best ways to get ideas to write about is just by paying attention to all the things that happen to them throughout the day. Explain that when something happens that gives them an idea for a topic to write about later, they should jot it down on a sticky note and put it in a "parking lot" for later use.

You need to model this strategy for your students. Periodically, as you think of a possible writing topic, write it down on a Post-it note and "park" the note on the parking-lot poster.

Maybe one morning things are particularly busy as you're getting ready to come to school. You get to school that morning and you tell your students, "The craziest things happened this morning while I was getting ready for school. In fact, I think I might just want to write about some of these things. They'd probably make a funny story. So I'm going to put 'My busy morning' on the parking-lot poster to remind me that this is something I might want to write about later." (Walk to the poster and write that down as you're talking.)

Then find a five-minute time later that day or another day and write in front of your students about that busy morning (or any of the other topics you've written down). You'll be modeling your enthusiasm for writing as well as encouraging students to keep that parking-lot topics list going.

Practice: Now that you've demonstrated how to use the parking lot, it's time for the students to try it on their own.

- Give each student a copy of the reproducible to keep in a writing folder.
- Ask each student to jot down his own writing ideas on his "parking lot" paper.
- Whenever a student has time during the day, he can write about one of his topics.

THE TRAIT OF IDEAS

Just the Right Size

Purpose: When students write, they often try to write about topics that are way too broad to let them include specific, high-quality details. Don't they just love to write those dawn-to-dusk stories? Once a third grader told me he was going to write his one-page report on ancient Egypt! This lesson helps students narrow their topics so they're more manageable.

Materials & Preparation: You'll need four coat hangers, one package of clothespins, and the "Just the Right Size" reproducible on page 100. Make enough enlarged copies of the reproducible so that every four students in the class can have one set of four T-shirts and you have one extra set for modeling. It's a good idea to use a different color of cardstock for each set, to make it easier to keep track of them. Cut out the T-shirts.

Now pick the groups of words or phrases you want to use—these can be the ones on page 45 or you can substitute your own. Write one of the words or phrases on each of the cut-outs, being careful to keep all the pieces of each set on shirts that are all the same color.

Next, create four labels for the coat hangers. One should say "Extra Large," one "Large," one "Medium," and one "Small." Put one label on each of the coat hangers.

Model: Say to your students something like this: "Have you ever tried on clothes and the sizing just didn't work? Sometimes in stores, clothes get all out of place on the size racks. Let's pretend you wear a size small. Sometimes you might think you're getting your correct size, but when you try it on you find out it's an extra large and it's just too big for you. So you go get another size, and again, it's the wrong size. You've brought a size large into the dressing room.

"So you go back to the rack and find a size medium, but that *still* isn't right. Finally you locate a size small. You try it on and it's just the right size.

A Quick Tip

If you want to make this lesson truly novel, bring in actual clothing in the four sizes. That's an experience the students will remember!

"Well, it's like that in writing. Size small is the best fit for your writing topic; a small is just the right size. So let's play a game and see if we can find the small size each time."

Next, let's say each of the T-shirts you've chosen for modeling has one of these topics written on it:

- Sports
- Baseball
- Attending a Major League Game
- The Time I Caught a Foul Ball

Now think aloud for students as you "hang your clothes" on the appropriate hangers, using clothespins for each one. The illustration at right shows how your "wardrobe" should look.

Emphasize to students that the topic on the small hanger is just the right size for writing.

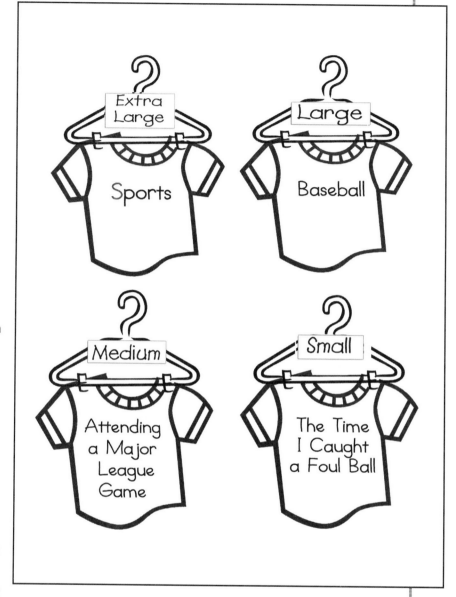

Practice: Before starting this activity, separate the students into groups of four.

- Pass out one set of "clothes" to each group.
- Have students discuss the sizes of what they've been given.
- Ask each group to come to the front of the room and pin their "clothes" on the appropriate coat hangers, telling the rest of the class why they made the decisions they did.

Possible Labels for the "Clothes"

Set #1
- State
- City
- My House
- My Bedroom

Set #2
- Living Room
- Table
- Table Top
- Flower Arrangement on Table Top

Set #3
- Shopping
- Department Store
- Jewelry
- The Pearl Necklace

Set #4
- Pets
- Dogs
- Taking Care of a Puppy
- Teaching a Puppy to Sit

Set #5
- Florida
- Orlando
- Disney World
- Space Mountain Ride

Set #6
- Kitchen
- Refrigerator
- Lunch Meats
- Spoiled Turkey

Set #7
- Weather
- Hurricane
- Strong Winds
- Hiding in the Hall Closet During the Storm

Set #8
- School
- Fourth Grade
- Our Classroom
- My Desk

Answers for Just the Right Size

Extra Large: State, Living Room, Shopping, Pets, Florida, Kitchen, Weather, School

Large: City, Table, Department Store, Dogs, Orlando, Refrigerator, Hurricane, Fourth Grade

Medium: My House, Table Top, Jewelry, Taking Care of a Puppy, Disney World, Lunch Meats, Strong Winds, Our Classroom

Small: My Bedroom, Flower Arrangement on Table Top, The Pearl Necklace, Teaching a Puppy to Sit, Space Mountain Ride, Spoiled Turkey, Hiding in the Hall Closet During the Storm, My Desk

THE TRAIT OF IDEAS

Binoculars

Purpose: This mini-lesson is adapted from a strategy in one of Barry Lane's books, *The Reviser's Toolbox*. It's a great way to help your students add those quality details to a piece of writing.

Materials & Preparation: A trip to your local dollar store can make this lesson really come alive. Buy a pair of the binoculars that most of those stores carry and you're all set.

Model: Discuss with your students why a person would want to take a pair of binoculars somewhere (to see better). Ask students what has to be done to see better using a pair of binoculars (you have to turn the knobs to focus them). Then tell your students that writing is just like that. Whenever students want to add specific details to their writing, they need to ask themselves what questions the reader would want to have answered. Each time they ask a question, it's like turning the knobs on those binoculars and bringing things into focus.

Now, go to your overhead, face your students, and write this sentence: "The airplane was new." Give the pair of binoculars to a student and ask the student to start "turning the knobs on the binoculars," helping you to bring details into your writing by asking questions that the student would like to have answered about that airplane. The student might ask:

- What color is the plane?

- How big is it?

- How fast can it go?

- How many people can it hold?

Then start writing, making sure you answer those questions. Your sentence might now read: "The sleek, silver plane with bright blue trim and a wingspan of 199 feet can comfortably hold 283 people and cruise at 550 miles per hour." Wow! Just by asking some questions and then answering them in the writing, you've turned a rather boring sentence into one that is full of specific details.

Practice: Students need to know that the more they turn the knobs of the binoculars (the more questions they can think of that the reader would want answered, and the more they focus on answering those questions), the more their writing will be improved by those specific, high-quality details. Here's a way to get them started.

- Give students a boring sentence such as one of these:
  - » The dog was funny.
  - » My desk is a mess.
  - » I like my cat.

> » I got a new bike.

> » We went to a movie.

> » There is a rocking chair by the fireplace at my house.

> » A famous person just walked into our classroom.

- Pair up students and let them practice asking each other questions about the topics of the sentences. Tell them to see if they can come up with more specific details they could add to make the sentences more interesting.

- Once you've introduced this strategy, challenge your students to remember the binoculars whenever they're stuck in their writing. Tell them to pretend they have binoculars and to start "turning those knobs"—using their writing to provide answers to questions their readers might ask. This will help them get past the "fuzziness" in their writing as they learn to see, hear, taste, touch, and smell the details.

For Example

Here's a sample from a student who was asked about a memory from the first week of school. Her memory was "getting in trouble." Her partner for the practice activity began asking her questions about that memory and she responded in her writing. Look at how her writing became more focused as she added specific details—and note that she bit her mother!

Memory: Getting in Trouble

Details: My mom throw water on me. cause I Bit her. She was mad at me. I Bit her because she yelled at me. she yelled at me because I had an atitude. I had an atitude because I couldn't go out an play. I had homework.

THE TRAIT OF ORGANIZATION

Double D/Double T

Purpose: This lesson helps students learn to write more effective leads.

Materials & Preparation: Make a poster-size copy of the "Double D/Double T" reproducible on page 101. Make one copy for each student of the "Practice with Leads" reproducible on page 102.

Model: Using the poster as a reference, tell students that Double D/Double T is an easy way to remember different approaches they can use for leads. Explain what each of the letters stands for (D is for description and dialogue or question; T is for thought and tension or a powerful statement) and share with students the examples from the poster.

Now model how to use this approach. Write a boring lead on your overhead—maybe something like: "I am going to tell you how I survived on a remote island for five days." Then show students ways to revise that lead, using each kind of Double D/Double T approach. For example, using the dialogue-style lead (remember that it can also be a question), you might come up with something like this: "Have you ever had a nightmare about being stranded all by yourself on some uncivilized island? I, unfortunately, experienced this nightmare in real life!"

Practice: Tell students they can refer to the Double D/Double T poster if they need to "jog their memories."

- Give one copy of the "Practice with Leads" reproducible to each student.
- Have each student choose a topic and then write four different leads for it, one using each of the Double D/Double T approaches.

Description

The writer begins by establishing the setting of the writing and creating a picture in the mind of the reader.

Example, from *Ralph S. Mouse,* by Beverly Cleary: "Night winds, moaning around corners and whistling through cracks, dashed snow against the windows of the Mountain View Inn."

Dialogue or Question

The writer begins with a few lines of dialogue or with a question.

Example, from *Charlotte's Web,* by E.B. White: "'Where is Papa going with that ax?' said Fern to her mother as they were setting the table for breakfast."

Thought

The writer begins with a thought inside a character's head.

Example, from *The Color of Water,* by James McBride: "As a boy, I never knew where my mother was from—where she was born, who her parents were."

Tension or Powerful Statement

The writer begins with a forceful statement or words that leave the reader wanting more.

Example, from *The True Story of the Three Little Pigs,* by Jon Scieszka: "Everybody knows the story of the Three Little Pigs. Or at least they think they do. But I'll let you in on a little secret. Nobody knows the real story, because nobody has ever heard my side of the story."

Read for Leads

Challenge students to look in their reading for leads that illustrate any of the Double D/Double T approaches. Ask them to write down the source for each lead and the lead itself. You might post these on a Double D/Double T bulletin board in the classroom.

THE TRAIT OF ORGANIZATION

Beyond "The End"

Purpose: This strategy helps students understand how they can write effective conclusions.

Materials & Preparation: Make a poster from the "Types of Conclusions" reproducible on page 103 and hang the poster in your classroom. Then make one copy of the "Practice with Conclusions" reproducible on page 104 for each student.

Model: Explain the types of conclusions listed on the poster. Then, using a sample of your own writing, work with the students to model ways to create more effective conclusions, demonstrating each approach shown on the poster. For example, you might write, "I rode away on my bike." To revise with a summary/reflection conclusion, you could write, "As I pedaled my bike down the winding streets of the small village, I knew I would always treasure the summers I had spent in the cottage by the shore." Then you would continue with examples of the other types of conclusions.

Practice: Have students pair off for this activity.

- Give each student a copy of the "Practice with Conclusions" reproducible.
- Explain that each pair is to write two new, more effective conclusions for that story, each using one of the types of conclusions shown on the poster.

THE TRAIT OF ORGANIZATION

Mix It, Fix It

Purpose: This lesson helps students focus on all the elements of organization: leads, transitions, and conclusions.

Materials & Preparation: Start with "The Power of a Flower" reproducible on page 105. On cardstock, make one copy for every four students in the class. (You might want to use a different color for each copy.) Cut the sentences into strips, laminate them, and place each set of strips in a resealable plastic bag. Turn to the answer-key reproducible on page 106 and again make one copy for every four students. Set the answer keys aside for now.

Model: Write four sentences on an overhead transparency. You might use some like these:

- "He likes to run and chase squirrels."
- "Whenever he gets a chance, he loves to be outside."
- "Rocky, the dog, is a house dog."
- "Also, he likes to bark at the neighbor's dog."

Cut each sentence into a separate strip, and then place the strips on the overhead in random order. Think aloud as you rearrange them in an order that makes sense. Be sure to emphasize *why* you're putting the sentences in the order you've chosen.

Practice: Before beginning this activity, divide the students into groups of four.

- Give each group a set of the strips from "The Power of a Flower."
- Have each group work together to put their strips in order.
- As each group finishes, hand those students a copy of the answer key and have them check their answers. You may find that some students place the strips in an order that's different from what the author used. That can be okay. The important thing is that students are able to justify the order they chose.

A Quick Tip

This strategy can be used with all modes of writing, although it's easiest to apply it to short stories. To add some spice, throw in a line that doesn't fit at all. The point is to get a discussion going with students so they can verbalize why they chose the order they did.

R.A.F.T. (Role-Audience-Format-Topic)

Purpose: R.A.F.T. is a writing strategy that can be used to encourage creativity in all content areas. It also adds voice to writing because it requires students to write from different points of view.

Materials & Preparation: The only materials you need for this lesson are samples of R.A.F.T.s. To come up with those, it helps to know what they are! R.A.F.T. stands for Role, Audience, Format, and Topic. So a R.A.F.T. assignment might be for a student to pretend she's a plant writing a thank-you note to rain explaining how rain helps the plant grow. The role is the plant, the audience is the rain, the format is the thank-you note, and the topic is how rain helps the plant grow.

You can generate your own R.A.F.T. examples or you can turn to either of two excellent resources cowritten by Ruth Culham and Amanda Wheeler. One is *Writing to Prompts in the Trait-Based Classroom: Literature Response;* the other is *Writing to Prompts in the Trait-Based Classroom: Content Areas.*

Model: Here's a great way for you to model a R.A.F.T. for your students and at the same time demonstrate how you think as you write.

Explain that in this case, you're defining R.A.F.T. this way:

- R(ole): a student desk
- A(udience): a typical student in the grade level you teach
- F(ormat): advice
- T(opic): keeping your desk neat

Okay, go for it! Try it now. Get a blank sheet of paper and start writing. Give advice from a desk to a student on keeping a desk neat. Once you see where this exercise takes you, you'll be ready to write in front of your students.

Practice: This is a great way to build an understanding of voice.

- Find a story to read aloud to your students. Let's say you use "Eleven" from Sandra Cisneros's *Woman Hollering Creek*. Ask students to do a R.A.F.T. around this story as follows:

  » R(ole): Mrs. Price

  » A(udience): herself

  » F(ormat): journal entry

  » T(opic): what happened in school today

- After giving students time to complete their R.A.F.T.s, allow several to share their writing aloud. They will hear different "voices" of Mrs. Price.

THE TRAIT OF VOICE

Can You Feel It?

Purpose: This lesson connects the trait of voice to the feelings good writing evokes in the reader.

Materials & Preparation: Make a list of feeling words and write each word on an index card. Include words such as "happy," "sad," "excited," "nervous," "scared," "bored," "frustrated," and "calm." You'll need one card for every four students in the class. Then make a placemat to go with each card: draw a large circle in the middle of a sheet of bulletin-board paper and section it off as shown in the illustration.

Model: On an overhead transparency, write a word that describes feelings in a boring way. Let's say you write the word "happy." Explain to students that the key to the trait of voice is feelings. When writing contains a strong voice, that voice comes through because the writer really cares about the topic; as a result, the writing usually evokes some kind of feelings in the reader. Tell students that if you just write "I am happy," that doesn't cause the reader to feel much of anything. The writer needs to make "happy" come alive by being more specific.

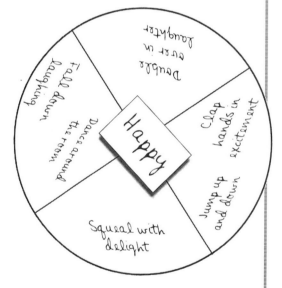

Next, guide students in brainstorming a list of things a person might do if he's happy. You might list things like:

- Double over in laughter
- Jump up and down
- Squeal with delight
- Dance around the room

Lead students to discover that the more feelings they can show in their writing, the more their voices will come through.

Practice: Before beginning this activity, divide students into groups of four.

- Give each group a blank placemat and one of the index cards you've prepared.
- Have each group place its card in the center of the circle on the placemat.
- Working simultaneously and independently, each student writes on her section of the placemat some ideas for describing the boring word for a feeling. Explain that she's to come up with words that would make the reader really understand the feeling. Allow five minutes for individual work.
- Within each group, students take turns sharing their descriptions of the group's feeling word.
- Each group picks out three or four of the group's favorites to share with the class.

Remove the Boredom

Ask each student to take out a piece of writing that he's currently working on and scan it for feeling words that are boring. Ask students to revise their work by adding more descriptions to make the feelings come alive for the reader. By doing this, they'll be adding voice to their writing.

THE TRAIT OF VOICE

Talk on the Phone or Write a Letter

Purpose: This lesson gives students another approach to adding voice to writing, as they pretend they're communicating in some other way.

Materials & Preparation: None

Model: Explain to students that one way to add voice to writing is to pretend you're talking on the phone or writing a letter. To illustrate, write on the overhead a sentence that has no voice, just information. Maybe you write: "My teenage son doesn't drive very well."

Now rewrite the sentence for the students—twice. The first time you rewrite it, pretend you're talking on the phone to your best friend. The second time pretend you're writing a letter to that same friend. Discuss with students how the voice really comes out when you use this approach.

I know you want an example here of what this might look like, but I'm not going to give you one. After all, I don't want you just copying what I write. I want you to write it! Go ahead, try it out—you can do it!

Practice: Provide your students with a prompt that is lacking voice. You might choose something like this: "My friend Mary never does her homework."

- Explain that you want each student to rewrite the sentence in one of two ways: by pretending she's talking on the phone to her best friend or by writing a letter to that friend.
- Let students share their writing. Discuss with them how voice seems to emerge when they use either technique.

THE TRAIT OF WORD CHOICE

10 Steps to Better Word Choice

Purpose: One of the characteristics of good word choice is the use of lively verbs. This lesson helps students select more lively verbs.

Materials & Preparation: None

Model: Tell students you're going to write 10 sentences on the topic of "family," but you're going to try not to repeat a word once you've written it. If you use the word "family" or the word "the" or the word "is" in the first sentence you write, you may not use that word again in another sentence. Then model this.

Practice: Now that they've seen you do it, it's time for students to try this on their own.

- Give students a topic such as "friends" and challenge each student to write 10 sentences without repeating a word once it is used.
- Ask them to stand when finished.
- When most of the students are standing, have several read their sentences while the rest of the class listens for any repeated words.
- The students will discover that this activity helps them really think about the verbs they're using. What most often happens is that students use verbs such as "is," "are," "was," and "were" early on and then have to pick more lively verbs to get 10 sentences completed.

A Quick Tip

To encourage students to use more lively verbs, create a classroom word wall of lively verbs that students can use in their writing.

THE TRAIT OF WORD CHOICE

Creating Word Images

Purpose: This lesson helps students use words that invite the reader to see, hear, smell, feel, or taste specific things.

Materials & Preparation: Turn to the "Creating Word Images" reproducible on page 107. Make one copy for each student, plus one overhead transparency.

Model: Select an object to write about. For example, let's say you choose to write about a pillow. Model on the overhead how you would fill in the blanks of the reproducible based on the word "pillow." Then discuss with students which images they like the best of the ones you created.

Practice: Before you begin this activity, give each student a copy of the reproducible.

- Ask each student to look around the classroom and select an object to describe.
- Have everyone complete his copy of the reproducible.
- Ask several students to share their writing and tell which images they liked the best in what they wrote.

CREATING WORD IMAGES

My Object: _a pillow_

The _pillow_ looks like a _marshmallow_.

The _pillow_ sounds like _a whisper_.

The _pillow_ feels like _a giant cotton ball_.

The _pillow_ tastes like _straw_.

The _pillow_ smells like _sleep_.

One thing about this _pillow_ is _that its lumpy!_

THE TRAIT OF WORD CHOICE

Fabulous Five

Purpose: This strategy helps students choose precise nouns.

Materials & Preparation: None

Model: On an overhead transparency, write a general noun. Let's say you write the word "child." Then model for students the process of coming up with five nouns that are more precise versions of your original one. You might list words like "baby," "infant," "toddler," "pre-schooler," and "tot."

Practice: Invite students to work in pairs for this activity.

- Give students a list of general nouns like these:

    Cat   Sports   Sound   Food   Candy   Pet

- Ask each pair to come up with five more precise nouns for each general one.

More Practice

Ask each student to get out a piece of writing she's currently working on and circle all the general nouns she finds. Invite students to revise their work by substituting more precise nouns for the general ones.

THE TRAIT OF SENTENCE FLUENCY

Tally It Up

Purpose: This lesson helps make students aware of the critical parts of sentence fluency: variation in the ways sentences begin and variation in the general patterning of the sentences. When you teach this lesson, you can also remind students to use those lively verbs that are an important part of the trait of word choice.

Materials & Preparation: Turn to the "Tally It Up" reproducible on page 108. Make one copy for each student and one overhead transparency.

Model: Start with a piece of your own writing. (It doesn't have to be perfect. The point is to show students how they can *improve* their writing!) Model for students how to fill in the reproducible by listing the beginnings of sentences and the verbs in each sentence, then counting the number of words in each sentence.

Point out that if many or all of the sentences begin with the same words, or if the sentences are pretty much all the same length, then perhaps revision is in order. Also explain that if the verbs seem to be "dead" or overused verbs, then substituting more lively verbs would improve the writing.

Practice: This is an activity for each student to complete individually.

- Ask each student to get out a piece of her own writing.
- Give each one a copy of the "Tally It Up" reproducible.
- Have each student complete the work sheet based on the writing selected.
- Ask each student to share the results with a partner.

TALLY IT UP

Sentence Beginnings	Verbs	Number of Words
First you need	need	6
Second you need	need	18
Third you study	study	10
Some are	are	9

THE TRAIT OF SENTENCE FLUENCY

Variety Is the Spice of Sentences

Purpose: This lesson shows students several ways they can vary sentence structure to make their writing more interesting.

Materials & Preparation: None

Model: On an overhead transparency, write a sentence. You might write, "The shell calmly washed up on the shore." Then show students different ways of rewriting the sentence.

Practice: Now it's time for the students to try this strategy on their own.

- Give your students a sentence and explain how it's structured.
- Ask them to try writing the sentence in different ways.

For Example

For a starting sentence such as "The shell calmly washed up on the shore," you might demonstrate some of these variations.

Rewritten as a question: Did the shell calmly wash up on the shore?

Rewritten as an exclamation: How calmly the shell washed up on the shore!

Rewritten using an adverb first: Calmly, the shell washed up on the shore.

Rewritten with a prepositional phrase first: On the shore, the shell washed up calmly.

Rewritten using a quotation: The boy explained, "The shell calmly washed up on the shore."

THE TRAIT OF SENTENCE FLUENCY

Combine It

Purpose: This lesson helps students combine short, choppy sentences into longer, more interesting ones.

Materials & Preparation: None

Model: Write the following sentences on an overhead transparency:

I have a new baby sister.

Mom went to the hospital early yesterday.

The baby was born late last night.

Her name is Sarah.

Now rewrite the same information for students as one sentence: "After going to the hospital early yesterday, my mom gave birth to my new baby sister, Sarah, late last night."

Practice: If you like, use some of the samples below for this.

- Show your students several groups of sentences, one group at a time.
- Challenge each student to rewrite each group of short, choppy sentences as one longer sentence.
- Ask students to stand when they've finished.
- Once all the students are standing, let several of them share their sentences.

For Example

You might want to use these sample groups of sentences as a jumping-off point for your own examples.

I have a dog named Rocky. He eats all the time. He sleeps all the time. I love him.

My baby sister cries at night. Sometimes I can't go to sleep. I don't get up in the morning. I miss the school bus.

I am looking forward to the party. We will be able to meet the new neighbors. We can catch up on all the news.

The school is new. It has a big gym. It has lots of windows in the classrooms. There is a library with lots of books in it.

CAPS (Capitalization, Agreement and Usage, Punctuation, Spelling)

Purpose: This lesson helps students edit for one convention at a time.

Materials & Preparation: Start with four baseball caps, each a different color, and four pocket folders, one to match the color of each cap. Label the rim of one cap with a "C" for capitalization, one with an "A" for agreement and usage, one with a "P" for punctuation, and one with an "S" for spelling. Label each folder in the same way, making sure that the color of the folder matches the color of the corresponding cap.

In each of the first three folders, place a list of the rules (or examples of rules) the class has studied that fit that heading, or use copies of the reproducibles on pages 109–111. Hang the caps in the classroom writing area with the appropriate folder beneath each cap.

In addition, make a transparency of a writing sample. Once again, using your own writing works well for this and gets the students engaged.

Provide several pieces of the plastic elbow pipe plumbers use (available from home-building-supply stores) or a phonics phone (available from Crystal Springs Books). These are great tools for students to use when they're learning to edit for agreement, because as a student whispers into the phone or the elbow pipe, he can hear whether or not his writing sounds right. (This works best, of course, with students who've read or been read to a lot. They're better equipped to recognize what "sounds right.")

Model: Place the transparency of the writing sample on your overhead. Explain to students that when a piece of writing needs editing for more than one convention, it's often best to deal with one convention at a time.

Model taking out a sheet from the Capitalization folder (under the "C" cap) and using it as a guide to edit for capital letters first. Then replace that sheet in its folder and take out a sheet from the Agreement and Usage folder. Once again, model editing for just one convention, this time using the new sheet as a guide. Take your phonics phone or elbow pipe and model "whisper reading" your work into it.

Continue this process to edit for punctuation and then spelling.

Practice: Now students get a chance to apply what they've learned.

- Have each student pull out a piece of his own writing.
- Ask students to use the CAPS process to edit their writing for one convention at a time.

A Quick Tip

Note that I haven't included a "Spelling" reproducible. I'd suggest creating a list of words your students frequently misspell, then placing that in the Spelling folder.

THE TRAIT OF CONVENTIONS

Walk-Around Edit

Purpose: This strategy encourages your bodily-kinesthetic learners to *feel* rather than see needed punctuation.

Materials & Preparation: None

Model: Make up some "punctuation moves" to use to edit text while walking around the room. You might decide to stop to indicate a period, shrug your shoulders for a question mark, rock on your toes for a comma, and jump for an exclamation mark.

Then start reading a piece of writing aloud as you walk around the classroom. As you read, act out the punctuation in the text, following the moves you've invented. See if your students can guess what you're doing. (They might think you're crazy!)

Once they catch on to the general idea, teach them the specific punctuation "moves"— or invite them to invent their own!

Practice: This is a good way to get students up and moving with a purpose.

- Have each student pull out a piece of her own writing.
- Ask each student to perform (literally!) a walk-around edit of that writing.

Copyediting Symbols

Purpose: This lesson shows students how to use copyediting symbols. It is important for students to be aware of the symbols that many editors use in preparing work for publication. Teach those marks and encourage your students to use them in their editing.

Materials & Preparation: Turn to the "Marks for Editing" reproducible on page 112 and make one copy for each student.

Model: Using the copyediting symbols, edit some of your own writing for your students.

Practice: Students work individually on this activity.

- Give each student a copy of the reproducible for reference.
- Ask each student to select a piece of his own writing.
- Have students practice using the copyediting symbols to edit their text.

MARKS FOR EDITING

EDITOR'S MARK	PURPOSE	EXAMPLE
ℰ	Delete letter, word, sentence, line, or punctuation mark.	It was really cold.
∧	Add or insert letter, word, or sentence.	quickly He ran home.
≡	Change this lowercase letter to a capital letter.	Happy thanksgiving
/	Change this capital letter to a lowercase letter.	It's time for Dinner.
⌒	Combine these two words or parts of words.	To day is Thursday.
#	Put a space between two words.	Vanilla icecream is my favorite.

Rubrics & Self-Assessment

This is the most exciting part of using the traits of good writing in your classroom. Assessing the traits is really where the power of the traits lies. You want to put the ability to assess writing in your students' hands—not just in yours.

When I started teaching writing, I would assign writing and then assess what my students had written. The assessment consisted mostly of counting the number of words and using my red pen to do lots of editing. But assessment should *drive* your instruction, not come at the end of it.

That's what's so great about teaching the traits: As you use trait-based assessment in your writing classroom, your students learn that their *assessment* of their writing can drive their *revision* of their writing. Wouldn't that be a dream come true—students assessing and revising their own writing? Actually, using the traits of good writing is all about exactly that. Isn't that the icing on the cake—or the sauce on the ice cream sundae?

The good news is that students can learn to use assessment as the crucial link to effective revision. Using trait-based assessment means they'll learn to revise for one trait at a time. That makes the whole assessment/revision process so much simpler. It's not that all of the traits don't work together. They certainly do. But in trait-based assessment, you *teach* one trait at a time; your students learn to *assess* one trait at a time; and they learn to *revise* one trait at a time. Does that sound a whole lot more manageable than what you've been doing?

At this point you're probably wondering how all this assessment and revision is actually done. We'll save the revision piece for a later chapter; for now, let's focus on the assessment part.

The first step in assessment is to decide on a scoring or assessment rubric for each of the traits—a rubric your students can use all by themselves. That part's important. If the power of using the traits of good writing depends on your students' ability to assess their own writing, then it makes sense that the rubrics need to be in student-friendly language.

You may want to create your own rubrics or use another source, but for your convenience I've included six rubrics—one for each of the traits of good writing—at the end of this chapter. Each one is based on a baseball theme so your students can learn that they can score a single (1), a double (2), a triple (3), or a home run (4) on a particular trait.

Anything less than a home run (4) in the traits of ideas, organization, voice, word choice, and sentence fluency will need revision. Revision means the student is working to improve the *content* of the writing. The trait of conventions is different. Anything less than a home run (4) in *that* trait means the student will need to do some *editing*—of capitalization, agreement and usage, punctuation, and spelling—to make the writing correct.

As you begin to look at each of the rubrics in this book, notice how the language used to describe the scoring reflects the critical attributes of the trait. For example, the rubric for the trait of ideas (page 67) describes a single (1) as having a main idea that is not clear. The writing at this point lacks details and can confuse the reader. There is also unneeded information. A home run (4) in the trait of ideas would mean that the main idea is well developed, the content is clear and focused, and the writer includes an appropriate number of details to support her thinking.

Your students need to have copies of these rubrics (or whatever ones you decide to use) so they can refer to them. Consider making copies of the reproducibles on pages 116–21. You can run them off on different colors of cardstock or heavy paper, laminate each one, and punch a hole in the top corner of each. Give each student a book ring to hold the rubrics. As you teach each trait, give every student a copy of that trait's rubric to put on her ring. After you've taught all the traits, you might want to hand out copies of the reproducibles on pages 122–123.

A Quick Tip

As you're teaching your students how to assess writing samples, you might want to make enough copies of the "Signal Cards" reproducible on page 113 to give each student a set. Place each set in a resealable plastic bag and hand them out to your students. While they're assessing the traits, tell the class you want to know who thinks a particular piece of writing is more weak than strong or more strong than weak in a particular trait. Ask each student to hold up the card that indicates what he thinks. This lets you quickly see how many of your students "get it" and how many don't yet understand.

But you can't just decide on a rubric, pass it out to students, and expect them to start assessing their own writing immediately. You need to start collecting anonymous writing samples for students to practice assessing. They need to get used to the language of each rubric and learn how to assess a piece of writing for a trait without knowing who wrote it. It could be embarrassing and threatening to use writing from students currently in your classroom.

Where can you get anonymous writing? You can certainly use the overhead transparencies for the writing samples in the back of this book. You can also use writing from students you've taught earlier. One fun thing to do is to secure permission (see the reproducible on page 114) from former students to use their writing to teach future classes. Students feel so honored when you ask them to fill out an actual contract to use their writing. They like getting from you a copy of the contract that they can keep. Of course you'd make it a point to use these samples only as good examples of the traits. I'm sure you want to *encourage* your former students, not embarrass them.

Whatever your source, you might want to get a three-ring binder, index it by trait, and start putting overhead transparencies of writing samples into each section. Whatever samples you use, ask students to assess a trait in those samples only after you've taught that trait specifically, and you feel students have a handle on it.

A Quick Tip

Anonymity in writing samples is important at this stage—with one exception: *your* writing. Remember when we said earlier how important it is for you to write in front of your students? Trust me: they *love* to assess your writing!

Now I want you to look at each of the rubrics at the end of this chapter as well as the transparencies of student writing samples for each trait. I'm including with each writing sample an assessment for that specific trait plus teaching points to use with your students.

Of course, as you place each sample on the overhead, you'll want to cover the assessment lines at the bottom, at least until students have given their own assessments. But you may not want to uncover them at all. Remember: There's no one *correct* assessment for any piece of writing or for any trait. The key is to come up with a *defensible* assessment.

Don't worry if the writing samples provided are not from a grade level you teach. After all, the traits are the traits are the traits! It's perfectly okay to use samples with your students from grades other than the grade you're teaching. Also, just because I'm discussing a particular piece of writing in connection with a particular rubric, that doesn't mean you have to use the sample that way. Use that piece of writing to illustrate whatever trait you want! Once you are comfortable with the rubrics you're using and are familiar with the traits, you'll easily be able to decide which writing to use with which traits.

When your students first start assessing those anonymous samples, they may have a problem: Maybe they don't know where to start. If that happens, tell them to decide first if a particular piece of writing is more weak than strong or more strong than weak in that particular trait. Tell them that if they decide it's more weak than strong in that trait, then they're probably thinking a single (1) or a double (2). A decision of more strong than weak would probably mean a triple (3) or a home run (4).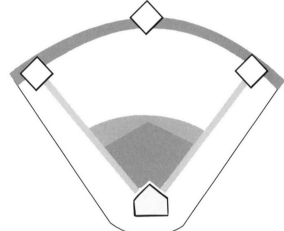

After you and your students decide if the writing is more weak than strong or more strong than weak in a particular trait, you can then begin to focus on each bullet point of the rubric. Let's say you decide the writing is more weak than strong in a particular trait. You could read each bullet point under the single (1) and if there's a clear match, then you might score the writing as a single. That's okay because you can tell your students that the writer "got on base." You always want to *encourage* students as writers, not discourage them.

If not every line under the single is a match, then go to the double (2) criteria. A perfect match would be a double (2). What if there are some criteria from a single that fit and some from a double that also fit? It's okay to have a score of 1+. Use baseball language and say, "Wow, almost a stand-up double, but not quite!"

Now, I bet I know what you're thinking: How will I know the correct score in a particular trait for an individual piece of writing? My answer to that is: Don't even try.

I've seen teachers use precious time and energy discussing whether a particular piece of writing is a 1 or a 2. Then the discussion can get negative and before you know it, the teachers are in the teachers' lounge participating in a good session of what I call the BMW club—bitch, moan, and whine.

Don't do that. Instead of agonizing over a *correct* score, think in terms of a *defensible* score. After all, if the score is anything less than a home run, revision and/or editing is needed. Wasn't that the point? As long as you can defend your assessment, you're okay. You're trying to help the writer improve the writing. Keep your focus on the writer!

Are you ready? Turn to the sample transparencies at the back of the book. Let's assess some student writing! Remember to start by deciding if the writing is more weak than strong or more strong than weak in the trait; then go from there to actually scoring the trait.

Once you and your students have had some practice assessing student writing, I hope both you and they will start to feel more comfortable with the traits. In the next chapter, we'll look at ways to help students *revise* their writing after they've assessed it.

RUBRIC FOR TRAIT OF IDEAS

Double (2)

- The main idea is here, but it needs work.
- At times the content is clear and focused.
- There are a few details.
- There is some unneeded information.

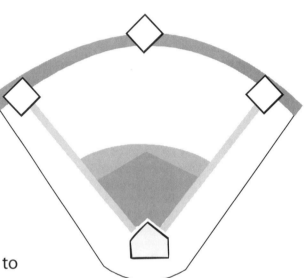

Triple (3)

- It's easy to tell what the main idea is.
- Most of the time the content is clear and focused.
- There are some good details.
- The reader still needs to figure things out.

Single (1)

- The main idea is not clear.
- The content is confusing.
- There are not enough details.
- There is a lot of unneeded information.

Home Run (4)

- The main idea is well developed.
- The content is clear and focused throughout.
- The writing includes the right number of appropriate details.

RUBRIC FOR TRAIT OF ORGANIZATION

Double (2)

- There is a weak writer's lead.
- Transitions are weak.
- There is some order, but the writing is confusing.
- There is a weak writer's ending.

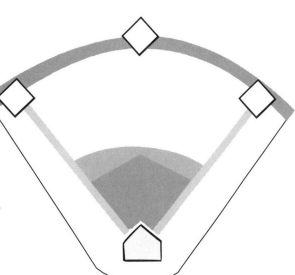

Triple (3)

- There is a writer's lead, but it could be better.
- Transitions are repetitive and sometimes don't work.
- At times the order makes sense, but not always.
- There is a writer's ending, but it needs to be more effective.

Single (1)

- There is no identifiable lead.
- Transitions are missing.
- The order of the details is random.
- There is no ending; the writing just stops.

Home Run (4)

- The writing has an effective writer's lead.
- There are smooth transitions that make the writing easy to follow.
- The order makes sense.
- There is an effective writer's ending.

RUBRIC FOR TRAIT OF VOICE

Double (2)

- Sometimes there is voice, and sometimes there is just information.
- The writing is distant, overly formal, or too informal.
- The writer can't seem to hit the right tone.

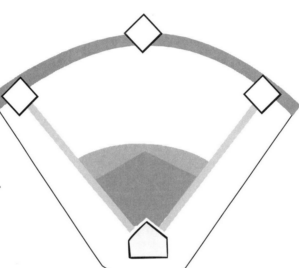

Triple (3)

- The voice is acceptable for the topic, audience, and purpose, but it doesn't bring the writing to life.
- The writing is pleasant, agreeable, and satisfying.
- Much of the time, the writer seems to care about the topic and the audience.

Single (1)

- There is no voice, only information.
- The writing is boring, stiff, and mechanical.
- The writer doesn't seem to care about the topic or the audience.

Home Run (4)

- The voice makes the writing come to life.
- The writing is lively, expressive, and engaging, with lots of energy.
- The writer really seems to care about the topic and audience, and it shows throughout the writing.

RUBRIC FOR TRAIT OF WORD CHOICE

Double (2)

- Some words are used correctly.
- Some verbs and nouns are strong, and some are ordinary.
- There is an over-reliance on passive verbs.
- The descriptions confuse the reader.

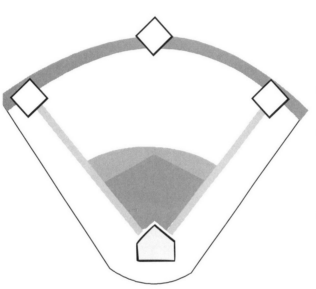

Triple (3)

- Most of the words are used correctly.
- Most verbs and nouns are strong.
- The words get the job done, but the writing is not there yet.
- At times, too much description buries the reader in details.

Single (1)

- The words are not used correctly.
- The writer uses limited and repetitive vocabulary.
- The words are colorless and flat. They fail to communicate.

Home Run (4)

- The words are fresh and unique. They make the message clear and memorable.
- There are strong nouns and lively verbs throughout.
- The writer creates clear mental pictures through effective words.

RUBRIC FOR TRAIT OF SENTENCE FLUENCY

Double (2)

- Most of the sentences begin the same way and are the same length.
- At times, the writing has to be reread to get the meaning.
- There are still inappropriate fragments and/or run-on sentences that interfere with flow.

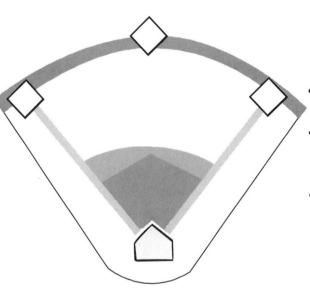

Triple (3)

- The writing can be read aloud but lacks enough rhythm and flow.
- Some sentences begin in different ways and are different lengths but are still basically simple sentences.
- In general, if there are fragments, they are used for a purpose.

Single (1)

- The writing is really hard to read aloud.
- The reader must stop and reread to get the meaning.
- The reader cannot tell where sentences begin or end because of run-ons and/or fragments.

Home Run (4)

- The writing is a joy to read aloud.
- The sentences vary in length and structure.
- Sentence structure, rhythm, and flow match the purpose.
- Fragments are used effectively.

RUBRIC FOR TRAIT OF CONVENTIONS

Double (2)
- There are errors that detract from the meaning.
- Some attention is given to capitalization, agreement and usage, punctuation, spelling, and paragraphing.
- Moderate editing would be needed to make this writing publishable.

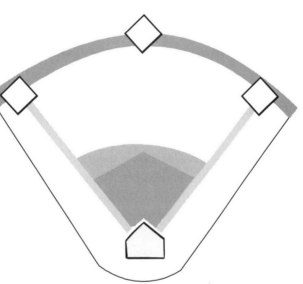

Triple (3)
- Some errors are present, but they do not detract from the meaning.
- Reasonable attention is given to capitalization, agreement and usage, punctuation, spelling, and paragraphing.
- Light editing would be needed to make this writing publishable.

Single (1)
- There are errors that interfere with meaning.
- No attention is given to capitalization, agreement and usage, punctuation, spelling, or paragraphing.
- Much editing would be needed before this writing would be publishable.

Home Run (4)
- The errors are so few that the reader can read right over them.
- Capitalization, agreement and usage, punctuation, spelling, and paragraphing are all excellent.
- The writing is virtually ready to publish.

Focused Revision

The single most powerful part of the six-trait system is using assessment to drive revision. And the great thing is that your students will be able to handle that assessment and revision themselves. If they can *assess* their own writing for a trait, then they'll be able to *revise* (or edit) their writing for that trait. Does that sound like a plan or what?

The key I want you to keep in mind is to teach students to revise for one trait at a time. Remember when I suggested to you that in editing, it's best to edit for one convention at a time? Well, the same holds true for revision. The real key to success in revision is to focus on just one trait at a time, revise for it, and then move on to another trait.

Of course, when you revise for one trait, you may automatically influence another. If a student is revising a piece of writing for the trait of ideas and trying to make the details more specific, he'll probably be revising for word choice as well. After all, it's careful and thoughtful word choice that helps make the details specific! The whole revision process is more manageable, however, when you revise for one trait at a time.

(By the way, this tends to be much easier for your students than it is for you. You may have spent years looking at all the traits at once. Your students don't have that history to "unlearn.")

Let's give it a try. I want you to read the following paragraph from a fourth grader and assess it for all six traits. That's right: all six. I would not ask you and you would not ask your students to assess for a trait if you hadn't taught the trait. You and I have looked at all the traits now, so go for it. Using the rubrics we've discussed, assess this text for all six traits.

Cathy

I have a friend. Her name is Cathy. She is special. She is the greatest friend. She is fun. She does fun things with me. I have a cat named Smokey. Cathy and I have been friends since second grade. She has lots of toys. She has a little brother. I have fun at her house. I hope we will be friends forever.

Trait	Score
Ideas	_____
Organization	_____
Voice	_____
Word choice	_____
Sentence fluency	_____
Conventions	_____

Okay, finished? How did you do? Most teachers give this one a 1 (single) or 2 (double) in each trait except for conventions; it usually gets a home run (4) there. I bet your scores were along those lines. Even if they weren't, though, remember: the important thing is not one *correct* answer, but rather a *defensible* answer. You will certainly agree that the writing isn't a home run in five of the traits. So at this point, this writing needs no editing (for conventions), but it does need revision for each of the first five traits.

This is where revising for one trait at a time becomes important. Which trait do you start with? It doesn't really matter, but often people like to start revision with the trait of ideas, just as they started writing with that trait.

To revise for the trait of ideas, I want you to think about some of the strategies you learned earlier for strengthening the ideas in a piece of writing. "Cathy" could be focused a little more. Remember the strategy from pages 43–45 for using coat hangers to hold topics of different sizes? With this particular piece of writing, the topic "Cathy" might be on the "large" hanger ("Friends" would be on the "extra large" one). Let's think about focusing on something appropriate for the "small" hanger. If "Fun Times Together" were on the "medium" hanger, then "Spending the Night at Cathy's House" might be on the "small" one. That topic would be just the right size.

That gets us to the topic of "Spending the Night at Cathy's House." At this point, the Binoculars strategy pages 46–47 might be a good one to use: that would mean providing answers to questions the reader would want answered about what happened the night the author stayed with Cathy. Using the Binoculars strategy would get the details more specific.

Once this writing is revised for the trait of ideas, you could then start revising for another trait. Always use the revised piece as the basis for the next round of revisions.

What Students Need from You

A great gift you can give your students is to provide specific approaches to improve the ways they use traits in their own writing. Whenever a trait is assessed as anything other than a home run, the student needs to either revise or edit for that trait. Students need specific ideas for revision for the first five traits and ideas for editing for the trait of conventions.

One way to model this process for your students is—you guessed it!—with your own writing. Here's a piece of writing I did for some fifth graders. It's a piece about something that happened in my family—something rather sad, but with a funny side to it. I'll explain that part in a minute. First take a look at the piece of writing, how the fifth graders assessed it, and the feedback they gave me about how to revise it.

The Day My Dog Died

My fifteen year old dog, Scruffy, died on September 16. It was sad. He was really sick so we decided to have him put to sleep. We knew he was not going to get well, and we thought he might be in a lot of pain. We got him when he was only six weeks old. My son, Paul, named him. The first owners called him Teddy, but Paul didn't like that. Anyway, my husband, Mr. Hollas, hugged him good-by and Scruffy was purring like a kitten. He used to always do that whenever Mr. Hollas hugged him like that. He never did that when I hugged him because I never could get the right hold. Anyway, I was trying to get out of the house as quickly as I could. It was my job to be the one to drive him to the vet where they would put him to sleep. I was trying not to look at my husband because I thought we both would cry. Beth Ann, our daughter, was away at college, so she had to say good-by on the phone to Scruffy. Anyway, I grabbed Scruffy and put him in the car and drove away. I talked to Scruffy and petted him in the car on the way. There were a lot of people in the vet's office so I had to wait for a few minutes. The nurse came to get him so I also had to say good-by. I paid the bill and was about to leave when the nurse came back and said that Scruffy was already dead when I brought him in! I was so shocked!

You're probably thinking, "How sad!" That's just what the students were thinking. Between you and me, though, there is a funny side to this. When I called my daughter, she said to me, "You took a dead dog to the vet?" (Remember the movie *Weekend at Bernie's?)* I didn't know he was dead, but believe me, once I found that out, I got a refund on the $30 I'd paid to have him put to sleep!

But let's get back to the students. I asked them to assess this piece based on the rubrics for ideas, voice, organization, and conventions (the traits the class was focusing on at the time). They gave me a double (2) in ideas and voice, a single (1) in organization, and a home run (4) in conventions. Some of their comments were quite interesting:

- "I bet you are sad and unstable."
- "You need a plan for organization."
- "Where's your voice?"
- "It's kind of boring now."
- "Revise the lead and conclusion."
- "Where are the transitions?"

According to the students' assessment, I didn't need to edit for conventions, but I definitely needed to revise for ideas, voice, and organization because none of those scored a home run (4).

The students felt I needed to work on organization first. I asked for suggestions on how I might revise for organization. They suggested a better lead, smoother transitions, and a more effective conclusion.

At this point you can think aloud as you start the revision process in front of the students; that way they can see exactly what you're doing as you're doing it. Or you can revise the piece later and then show them the revised copy. In this case we were short on time (that never happens to you, right?) so I revised it at home and showed the revised copy to the students later.

Then I asked the students which trait to revise next and we repeated the process. What I was modeling was *focused revision*: revising for one trait at a time. Each time I worked on a revision, I started with the revised copy from the previous round. Students began to understand that the revision process is much easier when the writer revises for one trait at time.

Let's go over a process for introducing your students to this type of revision.

1. Select a short piece of writing to share with your students. Use the "Cathy" reproducible on page 115 (a slightly longer version of the piece we assessed earlier in this chapter) or write a short piece of your own. Don't make it too strong! You want it to be weak in some of the traits. Make a copy of the writing sample for each student and make an overhead transparency as well.

2. Ask students to get out their rubrics and assess the writing. Explain which traits you want them to assess. If you've taught all six traits, the students can assess for all of them, but make sure they assess for one at a time. Encourage them to use the language of the rubrics when discussing their decisions. Get a class consensus for each trait.

3. If more than one trait requires revision, let the students discuss which trait they think needs to be worked on first.

4. Let students discuss possible ways to revise the writing for that particular trait. I like to have them work in pairs for this. The important thing is that the students revise for one trait at a time.

5. Have students share with the class their revised versions of the writing and then further revise for that trait—or move on to another trait and repeat the process. Be sure they remember to work each time from the last revised version of the copy.

6. Give blank overhead transparencies and pens to five or so pairs of students and ask them to copy their revised writing onto the transparency to be shared with the class. That way, students begin to understand there are many ways to revise for one trait.

Because you're modeling and giving students practice in revising for one trait at a time with others' writing, they'll eventually begin to apply what they've learned to their own writing. This is the goal: *for them to become independent assessors and revisers of their own writing.*

Remember

1. Always have students revise for one trait at a time.

2. Be sure they always start from the last revised version of the text.

Another way to put revision in the hands of your students is through the conversations you have with them as they're writing. You might call these conferences, but I like to think of them as conversations about the students' writing. To me, these conversations are one of the very best things about teaching writing. I don't remember ever having a conversation with one of my teachers about anything I'd written, but I wish I had. It's through the conversations you have with students that you can celebrate what they're creating in their writing, you can learn to know your students as writers, and you can find new opportunities to teach them about writing.

The best conversations occur when you just walk around your classroom as your students are writing, stopping for a few minutes to ask a student to read her writing to you and asking questions that invite student reflection. You might want to use questions such as these:

- "What's working for you?"
- "What's not working?"
- "What's this piece about?"
- "How can I help you?"
- "What's your favorite part?"
- "Why is this important to you?"
- "What are your next steps?"
- "How can you build on this idea?"

As you ask these types of questions, you'll be helping your students to develop as writers and putting assessment and revision in their hands.

Are you ready to begin your journey? The last chapter will help you get started on the right foot.

Getting Started

Now that you know six ways to teach the traits of good writing, you might be wondering how and where to start working these ideas into your teaching. I suggest that you *don't* start with the traits immediately. Teach the writing process first. Students need to know that writers pre-write, draft, share, revise, edit, and publish—not necessarily in that order or even always in the *same* order. They need to know that the process is very fluid and can get messy. They need to know that a writer can be working on several stages at once.

At the same time, you can be *getting ready* to teach the traits. Have you ever heard the saying, "Plan your work and work your plan?" There's a lot of truth in that! Much of your success in teaching the traits of writing depends on the planning and prep work you do. Here's a four-point checklist you might want to follow before you ever mention the traits in your classroom.

1. Start collecting writing samples that demonstrate good use of the traits. Save favorite books, newspaper clippings, magazine articles, catalog photos and descriptions, advertisements, and other copy you want to share with your students. Work with other teachers at your grade level to start one file for each of the traits. As each of you finds examples of writing you want to share with students, just put them in the appropriate files. Collecting examples and sharing with colleagues helps provide so many more resources to draw from.

2. Decide what rubrics your students will use to assess writing. You can have them use the ones in this book or you can create your own. It doesn't matter. The important thing is that, whatever rubrics you choose, you need to make copies and get them into your students' hands.

3. Begin to collect writing samples that your students can assess. These can be from previous students, from the works of published authors, from this book, and from your own writing. Not all of them should be home runs!

4. Often teachers at the same grade level like to get together and assess various pieces of anonymous student

A Quick Tip

Some teams of teachers like to store writing samples in their team offices in six crates, each crate a different color and labeled with the name of a different trait.

writing at their grade level to find "anchor" papers—models that show what they consider to be a home run for each trait for that grade. You might decide together that this is what you consider a "4" in ideas for a third grader, a "3" for a third grader, and so on. This gives your students specific examples they can use as guides as they start assessing their own writing.

Once students know the process and you've done your planning and prep work, you can introduce the traits of good writing. Use the ice cream sundae metaphor on pages 12–17 to give that overview, or take whatever approach is comfortable for you. Then you can start in-depth teaching with any of the traits.

Many teachers like to start with the trait of ideas because that's considered the foundation trait (remember the bowl of our sundae that holds all that ice cream!). But if you feel more comfortable starting with a different trait, then go for it! Teaching the traits of good writing is not a recipe or a "plan in a can." It's up to you to teach the traits in a way that you feel will help your students the most.

Teachers often ask me how long they should spend teaching each trait. I always say you should let your assessment of the needs of your students drive that decision. You might spend a week on one trait and a month on another. The time you spend on each one should be whatever your students require.

If you teach the writing process and then the traits, your students will have a solid foundation for learning about different modes of writing. This sequencing means that as you introduce new modes of writing, you can talk about how certain traits may be more important in some modes than in others. Voice, for example, is key in a personal narrative but may not be as important in technical writing.

A Quick Tip

If there's one guideline that's pretty universal, it's this: *teach all of the traits every year.* Some school faculties like to divide up the traits grade level by grade level. For example, in third grade the school may teach ideas and organization; in fourth grade, the school may teach voice. The problem with this approach is that all of the traits work together—and they can't work together if the students know only one or two of them. For that reason, all the traits need to be a part of writing instruction for every student every year.

Finally, I think congratulations are in order for you! You have now read about six ways to teach the traits of good writing to your students. I hope the ideas in this book will inspire you and help you to encourage independent writers.

I know that it can be uncomfortable and a little scary to start something like this in your classroom. You may have some misgivings about getting started, making the time, and planning for everything. If so, maybe this little story will help you. Whenever I think about taking a risk, I always remember a comment my daughter made to her dad when she was a teenager. She was dating a high school football player at the time and her dad asked her what position the fellow played on the team. My daughter responded, "I'm not real sure, but I think he's one of the drawbacks!"

I never wanted to be one of the "drawbacks" in my classroom. I know you don't want to be a drawback either—and you won't be if you always remember the critical part that you play as a role model in your writing classroom. As I suggested in the beginning of this book, you are the CEO (Chief Example for Others) in your writing class. The enthusiasm you show in your classroom will be contagious.

So go ahead now and get started on your exciting journey, teaching the traits of good writing to your students. If you get stuck along the way, go back and take another look at that ice cream sundae. Or *make* one and take a bite. Or—oh, go ahead and eat the whole thing! You wouldn't want it to melt!

Reproducibles

TRAIT SUNDAE

The Bowl: Ideas
The Scoops of Ice Cream: Organization
The Mix-Ins: Voice
The Toppings: Word Choice
The Syrups: Sentence Fluency
The Spoon: Conventions

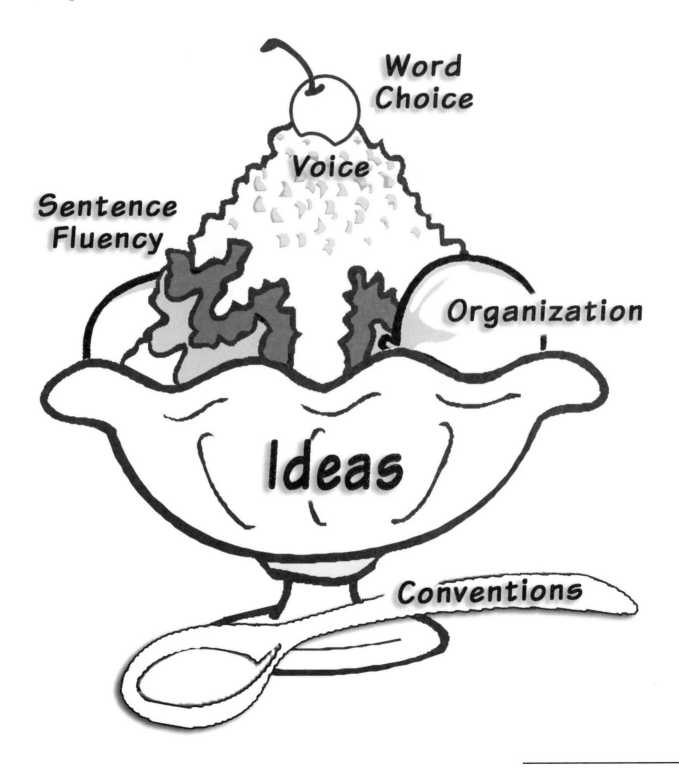

LOOK AT IDEAS THROUGH A MAGNIFYING GLASS

Clear message
Focused topic
Specific details
What is the purpose?
Who is the audience?

KEY WORDS & PHRASES

Ideas

- Clear message
- Focused topic
- Specific details

Organization

- Lead: grab attention
- Transitions: logical and linking
- Conclusion: tie it together

Voice

- Enthusiasm
- Involvement
- Feelings

Word Choice

- Words as pictures
- Precise nouns
- Lively verbs

Sentence Fluency

- Flow and rhythm
- Different sentence beginnings
- Different sentence lengths

Conventions

- Edit for CAPS (capitalization, agreement and usage, punctuation, spelling)
- Check the presentation

ALL ABOUT ME
(USING BLOOM'S TAXONOMY)

Knowledge

- *Define* yourself as if you were an entry in a dictionary.
- *Quote* your favorite book, movie, poem, or other passage.

Comprehension

- *Summarize* the events of your last school year.
- *Describe* your perfect day.

Application

- *Develop* a mission statement for the school for this year.
- *Relate* your interests outside school to one subject area in school.

Analysis

- *Compare* yourself to an animal.
- *Diagram* your dream house.

Synthesis

- *Collaborate* with another classmate to find out three new pieces of information about each other. Record the information you learn.
- *Compile* a list of adjectives that best describe you.

Evaluation

- *Persuade* your parents, in writing, to purchase an item you currently wish to own. Use exactly five sentences.
- *Make recommendations* as to what could make this a successful school year for you and the rest of the class.

CHARACTER-TAC-TOE

After reading a book and picking a character, choose three activities in the tic-tac-toe design. The three activities need to make a row horizontally, vertically, or diagonally. You may decide three activities are enough, or you may decide to keep going and complete more activities. You may work with one or more partners on one of the activities.

1 Write about a day in the life of your character.	**2** Create a collage that tells something about your character.	**3** Create a rap or song to describe your character.
4 Create a timeline of the important events in your character's life.	**5** FREE SPACE (your choice)	**6** With a group of three other students, write a fairy tale that includes your character.
7 Write a biography of your character.	**8** Write about how your character would react to winning the lottery.	**9** Write a poem that reveals your character's strengths and weaknesses.

I have chosen _____ (character)

from _____. (book)

I have chosen to complete these activities: #___, #___, and #___.

Student Signature: _____ Date: _____

Teacher Signature: _____ Date: _____

WRITING BINGO

Thank You Note	Wise Sayings	Poem	Fable	Movie Review
Recipe	Rhymes	Folk Tale	Bumper Sticker	Dream
Directions from One Place to Another	Memories	FREE SPACE (your choice)	Comic Strip	Lead
Rules for a Game	Dialogue	TV Commercial	Greeting Card	Conclusion
Wonderful Words	Puns	Opinion	Grocery List	Mystery

100 T.H.I.N.K. QUESTIONS

T (Thoughts/Feelings/Opinions/Points of View)

- How do you feel when no one laughs at your jokes?
- Which day of the week are you the happiest?
- What time of day is your favorite?
- What is your opinion of homework?
- What is your parents' opinion of homework?
- Be a baseball glove for one day. Tell what you do.
- If the number 4 could talk, what would it say?
- What would your journal say if it could talk?
- Pretend you are the principal. Describe your best day.
- How would you feel if you found out you were the teacher for one day?
- Be a pencil. Tell why you are better than a pen.
- Pretend you are (character from a book). What is your best (worst) memory?
- Pretend you are a dog. Who is your best friend?
- You are a trick question in math. What is the question?
- How do you feel when it's your birthday? (Answer from your birthday cake's point of view.)
- Two lockers are having a conversation. What are they saying?
- What would decimals say to fractions?
- You are the dumpster in an apartment complex. What surprises do you get every day?
- Do you ever feel sad when you laugh?
- Do you ever feel happy when you cry?

H (How Come?)

- How come the word "concentrate" is on an orange juice can?
- How come you recite at a school play and play at a music recital?
- How come a toaster has a setting that burns the toast?
- How come pushing the elevator button over and over again doesn't make it go faster?
- How come giraffes have spots but kangaroos don't?
- How come students don't have lunch duty?
- How come teachers send home papers with red marks and not yellow marks?

- How come you get in trouble for "talking back" to the teacher? Aren't you supposed to do that?
- How come a teacher can tell if a holiday is coming without looking at a calendar?
- How come Pluto is the only one who stands on all four legs if Goofy and Pluto are both dogs?
- How come you fill in a form by filling it out?
- How come there's not an egg in eggplant?
- How come boxing rings are square?
- How come you set your alarm to go off when you really want it to go on?
- How come water boils quickly unless you watch it?
- How come experience is the best teacher?
- How come a dog is a man's best friend?
- How come Barney is purple?
- How come you don't get smarter when you eat Smarties?
- How come a whole bag of light and fluffy marshmallows makes you gain weight?

I (What If?)

- What if the sun didn't exist?
- What if you only went to school on Saturdays?
- What if you lived where (name of a story) took place?
- What if computers didn't exist?
- What if your pet could talk?
- What if George Washington were still alive?
- What if all food tasted the same?
- What if there were no classroom rules?
- What if there were no chocolate?
- What if water didn't freeze?
- What if you awoke and you were 7 feet tall?
- What if there were no desks at school?
- What if water had an expiration date?
- What if you had eyes in the back of your head?
- What if you could travel at the speed of light?
- What if you could feel the earth rotating?
- What if you were invisible?
- What if there were no bananas?
- What if Columbus hadn't discovered America?

- What if your tongue were covered in glue?

N (Name and Next)

- Name all the ways you could say "Great!"
- A hurricane has destroyed the trees in your yard. What do you do next?
- Name all the ways you could communicate if you couldn't talk.
- Your dog begins to talk. What do you do next?
- The saying goes, "When in Rome, do as the Romans do." Name all the things you wouldn't do in Rome.
- Name all the things you wouldn't take on a camping trip.
- 1, 2, 3, 5, 8, 13, . . . What comes next?
- You are camping and drop your food in the river. What do you do next to get food?
- You are riding your bicycle and the tire goes flat. What do you do next?
- Name all the ways you can use a book.
- Name all the uses for a paper clip.
- Name all the good things about homework.
- You wake up during the night and smell smoke. What do you do next?
- Name all the ways you can think of to convince your friend to drink a glass of buttermilk.
- Name all the ways to use a toothpick.
- Name all the words you can make from the word "unbelievable."
- Name all the objects you can think of that are green and hard.
- Name all the reasons you can why it might be good to be early to something.
- Name all the questions you can add to this list of 100 T.H.I.N.K. questions.
- Name all the reasons you should be the principal for a day.

K (Kind of Alike and Kind of Different)

- How are a lunch box and a school alike?
- How are you different from your siblings?
- How are a piano and an elephant alike?
- How are a dog and a cat alike?
- How are a toothbrush and a comb alike?
- How is running the same as a ruler?
- How are you different from your parents?

- How are a racecar and the President alike?
- How are pictures and postcards different?
- How are risk and change alike?
- How is planning your weekend like solving a problem?
- How is gossiping about your friends like writing a story?
- How are an explorer and an artist different?
- How are last week and last month different?
- How are last year and today the same?
- How are school and a bagel alike?
- How are fireworks and candy canes alike?
- How are questions and answers different?
- How is school different from a party?
- How are people and vegetables alike?

WHO CAN'T PLAY?

List #1
One
Six
Ten
Banana
Seven

List #4
Happy
Sad
Confused
Joyful
Excited

List #7
Cat
Dog
Bird
Horse
Chicken

List #2
Policeman
Doctor
Teacher
Counselor
Plumber

List #5
Diary
Letter
E-mail
Postcard
Package

List #8
Glasses
Contacts
Hearing Aid
Braces
Band-Aid

List #3
Television
Computer
DVD Player
Cell Phone
Nintendo

List #6
Beach
Mountains
City
Country
Desert

List #9
Apartment
House
Tent
Office Building
Boat

CHALLENGE LINKS

Boy and Grab

LINK _____

New Words _____ _____

Man and Vane

LINK _____

New Words _____ _____

Rain and Black

LINK _____

New Words _____ _____

Day and Table

LINK _____

New Words _____ _____

Vase and Garden

LINK _____

New Words _____ _____

Library and Store

LINK _____

New Words _____ _____

Man and Nail

LINK _____

New Words _____ _____

Black and Cup

LINK _____

New Words _____ _____

Blown and Cuff

LINK _____

New Words _____ _____

Ball and Horse

LINK _____

New Words _____ _____

Under and Wrong

LINK _____

New Words _____ _____

Dirt and Rocky

LINK _____

New Words _____ _____

Dead and Back

LINK _____

New Words _____ _____

Kick and Moth

LINK _____

New Words _____ _____

Quartet and Shoe

LINK _____

New Words _____ _____

Answers to Challenge Links

Bag: Bagboy and Grab Bag
Weather: Weather Man and Weather Vane
Cloud: Rain Cloud and Black Cloud
Time: Daytime and Timetable
Flower: Flower Vase and Flower Garden
Book: Library Book and Bookstore
Hang: Hangman and Hangnail
Coffee: Black Coffee and Coffee Cup

Hand: Handblown and Handcuff
Fly: Fly Ball and Horsefly
Way: Under Way and Wrong Way
Road: Dirt Road and Rocky Road
End: Dead End and Back End
Ball: Kick Ball and Mothball
String: String Quartet and Shoestring

THE PARKING LOT

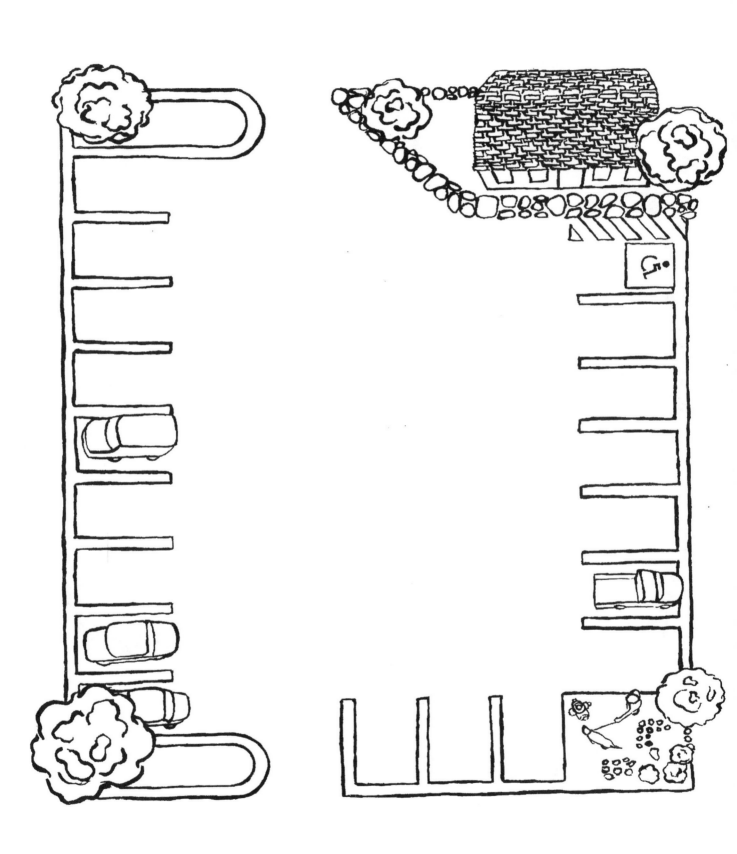

JUST THE RIGHT SIZE

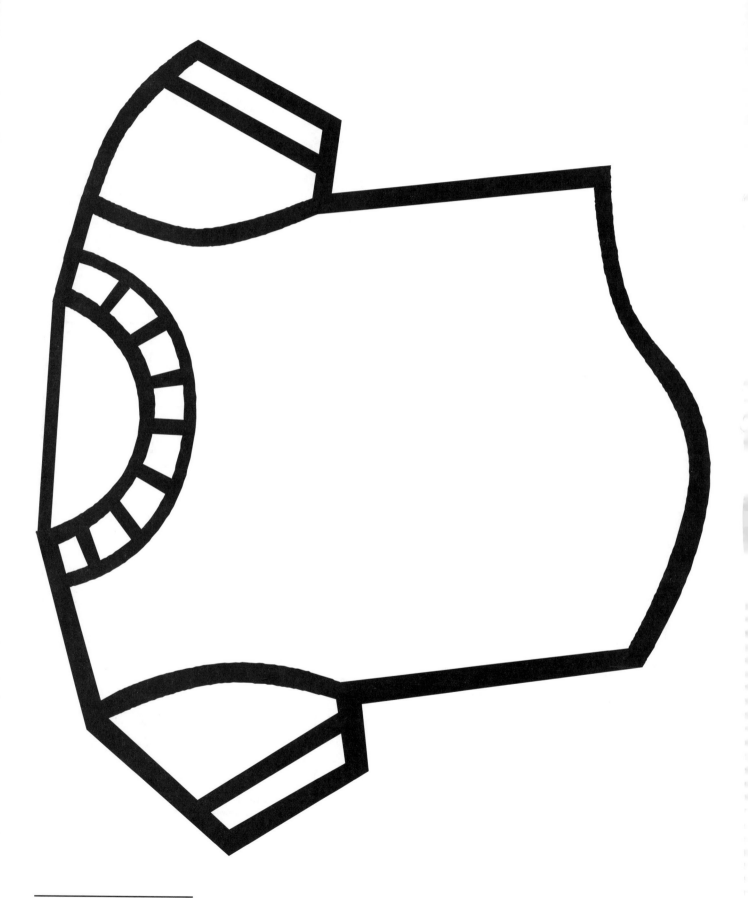

DOUBLE D/DOUBLE T

Description, Dialogue/Thought, Tension

Description

The writer begins by establishing the setting of the writing and creating a picture in the mind of the reader.

Example, from *Ralph S. Mouse,* by Beverly Cleary: "Night winds, moaning around corners and whistling through cracks, dashed snow against the windows of the Mountain View Inn."

Dialogue or Question

The writer begins with a few lines of dialogue or with a question.

Example, from *Charlotte's Web,* by E.B. White: "'Where is Papa going with that ax?' said Fern to her mother as they were setting the table for breakfast."

Thought

The writer begins with a thought inside a character's head.

Example, from *The Color of Water,* by James McBride: "As a boy, I never knew where my mother was from—where she was born, who her parents were."

Tension or Powerful Statement

The writer begins with a forceful statement or words that leave the reader wanting more.

Example, from *The True Story of the Three Little Pigs,* by Jon Scieszka: "Everybody knows the story of the Three Little Pigs. Or at least they think they do. But I'll let you in on a little secret. Nobody knows the real story, because nobody has ever heard my side of the story."

PRACTICE WITH LEADS

Choose a Topic

Choose a topic from this list or make up one of your own. Then try using the Double D/Double T strategy to write four different kinds of leads for the topic.

- My hair

- What I like (do not like) about shopping

- A book (movie) I like (do not like)

- Dogs

- (Pick your own topic.)

The topic I have chosen is: _____.

Write Four Leads

Lead with description: _____

_____

Lead with dialogue or question: _____

_____

Lead with thought: _____

_____

Lead with tension or powerful statement: _____

_____

TYPES OF CONCLUSIONS

The Circular Conclusion

This type of ending echoes the lead. Some suggested books for teaching circular conclusions are:

Tuck Everlasting, by Natalie Babbitt

Alexander Who Used to Be Rich Last Sunday, by Judith Viorst

On Call Back Mountain, by Eve Bunting

If You Give a Mouse a Cookie, by Laura Joffe Numeroff

Grandfather Twilight, by Barbara Berger

Barefoot: Escape on the Underground Railroad, by Pamela Duncan Edwards

Summary/Reflection

This type of ending repeats the main points of the writing or has a character reflecting on what has transpired. Books with conclusions based on summary or reflection include the following:

Green Eggs and Ham, by Dr. Seuss (summary)

The Twelve Days of Christmas (summary)

Harris and Me: A Summer Remembered, by Gary Paulsen (reflection)

The Emotional Conclusion

This type of ending can be happy, sad, mysterious, foreboding, humorous, or surprising. The following books have emotional conclusions:

Math Curse, by Jon Scieszka

The Best Christmas Pageant Ever, by Barbara Robinson

The Paper Bag Princess, by Robert N. Munsch

The Giver, by Lois Lowry

Stone Fox, by John Reynolds Gardiner

Unfinished Business

This type of ending leaves the reader wondering what will happen in the future. It can lead to a sequel. These books end with unfinished business:

The Indian in the Cupboard, by Lynne Reid Banks

Fantastic Mr. Fox, by Roald Dahl

PRACTICE WITH CONCLUSIONS

The Bike

Jack's mom would not get him a new bike. "Forget it," she told him. "Bikes cost way too much money. Besides, you need to earn your own money doing your chores. Then you can buy the bike."

One Saturday morning, when Jack went with his mom to the mall, he spotted a brand-new red bike in a store window. The bike was as shiny as a new penny and had great black stripes painted on it. The gears made it look like Jack could do lots of neat tricks while riding it. Jack just knew that the bike would be perfect for him.

He was just about to go into the store and see what he could find out about the bike when his mom came out of a store carrying two huge bags of things she had bought to take on a family camping trip. "Jack," she called. "Come and help me. What are you staring at, anyway?"

Write Two Conclusions

The short story above has no writer's conclusion. It just stops. Write two possible conclusions for the story, each using one of the following:

- The circular conclusion
- The emotional conclusion
- Summary/reflection
- Unfinished business

Ending One:

Ending Two:

Which ending do you like better?

THE POWER OF A FLOWER

How do these small flowering plants get up into a tall tree?

In those areas, trees often grow to be very tall.

There the seeds can sprout as they collect moisture from the tree.

It rains every day in some regions of the world.

 Seeds can get stuck in the bark of the tree.

Their leaves provide shade for the ground far below.

The orchid is an example of one of these flowers that
is part of a plant that lives in a tree.

Birds or other animals can drop seeds.

Some small flowering plants grow up in the trees so they can
get light instead of growing on the ground where it is dark.

 They can also get moisture from the air.

ANSWERS FOR "THE POWER OF A FLOWER"

- It rains every day in some regions of the world.

- In those areas, trees often grow to be very tall.

- Their leaves provide shade for the ground far below.

- Some small flowering plants grow up in the trees so they can get light instead of growing on the ground where it is dark.

- How do these small flowering plants get up into a tall tree?

- Birds or other animals can drop seeds.

- Seeds can get stuck in the bark of the tree.

- There the seeds can sprout as they collect moisture from the tree.

- They can also get moisture from the air.

- The orchid is an example of one of these flowers that is part of a plant that lives in a tree.

CREATING WORD IMAGES

My Object: _____

The _____ looks like _____.

The _____ sounds like _____.

The _____ feels like _____.

The _____ tastes like _____.

The _____ smells like _____.

One thing about this _____ is _____.

TALLY IT UP

Sentence Beginnings	Verbs	Number of Words

CAPITALIZATION RULES

George **W**ashington	*names of people*
Thanksgiving **D**ay	*holidays*
Empire **S**tate **B**uilding	*names of buildings*
Sunday	*days of the week*
January	*months of the year*
Main **S**treet	*names of streets*
Austin, **T**exas	*cities and states*
North **A**merica	*continents*
United **S**tates	*countries*
Dear **F**red,	*letter greeting*
Sincerely yours,	*first word in a letter closing*
A **W**rinkle in **T**ime	*titles (first and last words, and all important words in between)*
The sun dipped slowly.	*first word in a sentence*
"**W**e are here," Tim said.	*first word in a quote*

AGREEMENT & USAGE

No!	Yes!
He don't know.	He doesn't know.
Me and Mary are here.	Mary and I are here.
It was for me and Mary.	It was for Mary and me.
Can I go?	May I go?
Bring this to the office.	Take this to the office.

It was a dark and stormy night.

Will you help me?

I love ice cream!

I like apples, bananas, and pears.

"Wow!" she screamed.

"Yes, I am leaving now," said Sue.

Ken asked, "Where are you going?"

Seeing is observing what is before us; visualizing is imagining what might be.

MARKS FOR EDITING

EDITOR'S MARK	PURPOSE	EXAMPLE
ℒ	Delete letter, word, sentence, line, or punctuation mark.	It was really cold.
∧	Add or insert letter, word, or sentence.	quickly He ran home. ∧
≡	Change this lowercase letter to a capital letter.	Happy thanksgiving ≡
/	Change this capital letter to a lowercase letter.	It's time for Dinner.
⌒	Combine these two words or parts of words.	To day is Thursday.
#	Put a space between two words.	Vanilla icecream is my favorite.

MORE STRONG THAN WEAK

MORE WEAK THAN STRONG

AUTHOR'S CONTRACT
FOR PERMISSION TO USE WRITING

I, _____ , do give
(print author's first and last names)

_____ permission to make copies
(print teacher's name)

of my piece,_____ , to use as an
(print title of piece)

example of quality writing for future classes. I understand the

teacher will also copy the rubrics to use in discussing my piece

with future classes.

_____ (author's initials) **I do** give _____
(print teacher's name)

permission to use my name and the year of the writing's creation

when sharing my piece.

_____ (author's initials) **I do not** give

_____ permission to use my
(print teacher's name)

name and year of the writing's publication when sharing my piece.

Author's Signature: _____

Date Permission Given: _____

Teacher's Signature: _____

Date Contract Received: _____

WRITING SAMPLE FOR ALL TRAITS

Cathy

I have a friend whose name is Cathy. Cathy is special and the greatest friend. She is fun and a lot of fun to be with. She has a super personality and does fun things with me like going to the movies and sleeping over.

Cathy and I have been friends since we were in second grade. We became good friends right away. She had lots of toys and books at her house.

I like Cathy because she is cool and so is her family. We have fun when we are at each other's houses. I hope we will be friends forever.

RUBRIC FOR TRAIT OF IDEAS

Double (2)
- The main idea is here, but it needs work.
- At times the content is clear and focused.
- There are a few details.
- There is some unneeded information.

Single (1)
- The main idea is not clear.
- The content is confusing.
- There are not enough details.
- There is a lot of unneeded information.

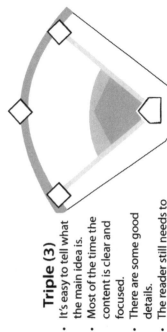

Triple (3)
- It's easy to tell what the main idea is.
- Most of the time the content is clear and focused.
- There are some good details.
- The reader still needs to figure things out.

Home Run (4)
- The main idea is well developed.
- The content is clear and focused throughout.
- The writing includes the right number of appropriate details.

RUBRIC FOR TRAIT OF IDEAS

Double (2)
- The main idea is here, but it needs work.
- At times the content is clear and focused.
- There are a few details.
- There is some unneeded information.

Single (1)
- The main idea is not clear.
- The content is confusing.
- There are not enough details.
- There is a lot of unneeded information.

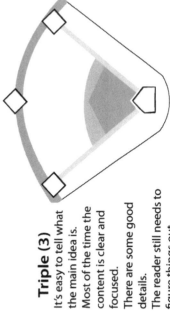

Triple (3)
- It's easy to tell what the main idea is.
- Most of the time the content is clear and focused.
- There are some good details.
- The reader still needs to figure things out.

Home Run (4)
- The main idea is well developed.
- The content is clear and focused throughout.
- The writing includes the right number of appropriate details.

RUBRIC FOR TRAIT OF ORGANIZATION

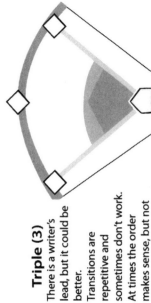

Double (2)
- There is a weak writer's lead.
- Transitions are weak.
- There is some order, but the writing is confusing.
- There is a weak writer's ending.

Single (1)
- There is no identifiable lead.
- Transitions are missing.
- The order of the details is random.
- There is no ending; the writing just stops.

Triple (3)
- There is a writer's lead, but it could be better.
- Transitions are repetitive and sometimes don't work.
- At times the order makes sense, but not always.
- There is a writer's ending, but it needs to be more effective.

Home Run (4)
- The writing has an effective writer's lead.
- There are smooth transitions that make the writing easy to follow.
- The order makes sense.
- There is an effective writer's ending.

RUBRIC FOR TRAIT OF ORGANIZATION

Double (2)
- There is a weak writer's lead.
- Transitions are weak.
- There is some order, but the writing is confusing.
- There is a weak writer's ending.

Single (1)
- There is no identifiable lead.
- Transitions are missing.
- The order of the details is random.
- There is no ending; the writing just stops.

Triple (3)
- There is a writer's lead, but it could be better.
- Transitions are repetitive and sometimes don't work.
- At times the order makes sense, but not always.
- There is a writer's ending, but it needs to be more effective.

Home Run (4)
- The writing has an effective writer's lead.
- There are smooth transitions that make the writing easy to follow.
- The order makes sense.
- There is an effective writer's ending.

REPRODUCIBLE PAGE

Double (2)
- Sometimes there is voice, and sometimes there is just information.
- The writing is distant, overly formal, or too informal.
- The writer can't seem to hit the right tone.

Single (1)
- There is no voice, only information.
- The writing is boring, stiff, and mechanical.
- The writer doesn't seem to care about the topic or the audience.

Triple (3)
- The voice is acceptable for the topic, audience, and purpose, but it doesn't bring the writing to life.
- The writing is pleasant, agreeable, and satisfying.
- Much of the time, the writer seems to care about the topic and the audience.

Home Run (4)
- The voice makes the writing come to life.
- The writing is lively, expressive, and engaging, with lots of energy.
- The writer really seems to care about the topic and audience, and it shows throughout the writing.

RUBRIC FOR TRAIT OF VOICE

Double (2)
- Sometimes there is voice, and sometimes there is just information.
- The writing is distant, overly formal, or too informal.
- The writer can't seem to hit the right tone.

Single (1)
- There is no voice, only information.
- The writing is boring, stiff, and mechanical.
- The writer doesn't seem to care about the topic or the audience.

Triple (3)
- The voice is acceptable for the topic, audience, and purpose, but it doesn't bring the writing to life.
- The writing is pleasant, agreeable, and satisfying.
- Much of the time, the writer seems to care about the topic and the audience.

Home Run (4)
- The voice makes the writing come to life.
- The writing is lively, expressive, and engaging, with lots of energy.
- The writer really seems to care about the topic and audience, and it shows throughout the writing.

RUBRIC FOR TRAIT OF WORD CHOICE

Double (2)
- Some words are used correctly.
- Some verbs and nouns are strong, and some are ordinary.
- There is an over-reliance on passive verbs.
- The descriptions confuse the reader.

Single (1)
- The words are not used correctly.
- The writer uses limited and repetitive vocabulary.
- The words are colorless and flat. They fail to communicate.

Triple (3)
- Most of the words are used correctly.
- Most verbs and nouns are strong.
- The words get the job done, but the writing is not there yet.
- At times, too much description buries the reader in details.

Home Run (4)
- The words are fresh and unique. They make the message clear and memorable.
- There are strong nouns and lively verbs throughout.
- The writer creates clear mental pictures through effective words.

RUBRIC FOR TRAIT OF WORD CHOICE

Double (2)
- Some words are used correctly.
- Some verbs and nouns are strong, and some are ordinary.
- There is an over-reliance on passive verbs.
- The descriptions confuse the reader.

Single (1)
- The words are not used correctly.
- The writer uses limited and repetitive vocabulary.
- The words are colorless and flat. They fail to communicate.

Triple (3)
- Most of the words are used correctly.
- Most verbs and nouns are strong.
- The words get the job done, but the writing is not there yet.
- At times, too much description buries the reader in details.

Home Run (4)
- The words are fresh and unique. They make the message clear and memorable.
- There are strong nouns and lively verbs throughout.
- The writer creates clear mental pictures through effective words.

RUBRIC FOR TRAIT OF SENTENCE FLUENCY

Double (2)
- Most of the sentences begin the same way and are the same length.
- At times, the writing has to be reread to get the meaning.
- There are still inappropriate fragments and/or run-on sentences that interfere with flow.

Single (1)
- The writing is really hard to read aloud.
- The reader must stop and reread to get the meaning.
- The reader cannot tell where sentences begin or end because of run-ons and/or fragments.

Triple (3)
- The writing can be read aloud but lacks enough rhythm and flow.
- Some sentences begin in different ways and are different lengths but are still basically simple sentences.
- In general, if there are fragments, they are used for a purpose.

Home Run (4)
- The writing is a joy to read aloud.
- The sentences vary in length and structure.
- Sentence structure, rhythm, and flow match the purpose.
- Fragments are used effectively.

RUBRIC FOR TRAIT OF SENTENCE FLUENCY

Double (2)
- Most of the sentences begin the same way and are the same length.
- At times, the writing has to be reread to get the meaning.
- There are still inappropriate fragments and/or run-on sentences that interfere with flow.

Single (1)
- The writing is really hard to read aloud.
- The reader must stop and reread to get the meaning.
- The reader cannot tell where sentences begin or end because of run-ons and/or fragments.

Triple (3)
- The writing can be read aloud but lacks enough rhythm and flow.
- Some sentences begin in different ways and are different lengths but are still basically simple sentences.
- In general, if there are fragments, they are used for a purpose.

Home Run (4)
- The writing is a joy to read aloud.
- The sentences vary in length and structure.
- Sentence structure, rhythm, and flow match the purpose.
- Fragments are used effectively.

REPRODUCIBLE PAGE

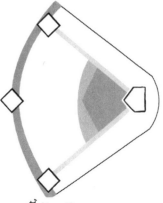

RUBRIC FOR TRAIT OF CONVENTIONS

Double (2)

- There are errors that detract from the meaning.
- Some attention is given to capitalization, agreement and usage, punctuation, spelling, and paragraphing.
- Moderate editing would be needed to make this writing publishable.

Single (1)

- There are errors that interfere with meaning.
- No attention is given to capitalization, agreement and usage, punctuation, spelling, or paragraphing.
- Much editing would be needed before this writing would be publishable.

Triple (3)

- Some errors are present, but they do not detract from the meaning.
- Reasonable attention is given to capitalization, agreement and usage, punctuation, spelling, and paragraphing.
- Light editing would be needed to make this writing publishable.

Home Run (4)

- The errors are so few that the reader can read right over them.
- Capitalization, agreement and usage, punctuation, spelling, and paragraphing are all excellent.
- The writing is virtually ready to publish.

RUBRIC FOR TRAIT OF CONVENTIONS

Double (2)

- There are errors that detract from the meaning.
- Some attention is given to capitalization, agreement and usage, punctuation, spelling, and paragraphing.
- Moderate editing would be needed to make this writing publishable.

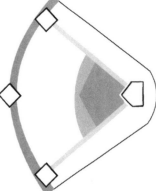

Single (1)

- There are errors that interfere with meaning.
- No attention is given to capitalization, agreement and usage, punctuation, spelling, or paragraphing.
- Much editing would be needed before this writing would be publishable.

Triple (3)

- Some errors are present, but they do not detract from the meaning.
- Reasonable attention is given to capitalization, agreement and usage, punctuation, spelling, and paragraphing.
- Light editing would be needed to make this writing publishable.

Home Run (4)

- The errors are so few that the reader can read right over them.
- Capitalization, agreement and usage, punctuation, spelling, and paragraphing are all excellent.
- The writing is virtually ready to publish.

6-TRAIT WRITING ASSESSMENT RUBRIC

| Trait | More Weak Than Strong | | More Strong Than Weak | |
	Single (1)	Double (2)	Triple (3)	Home Run (4)
IDEAS	• The main idea is not clear. • The content is confusing. • There are not enough details. • There is a lot of unneeded information.	• The main idea is here, but it needs work. • At times the content is clear and focused. • There are a few details. • There is some unneeded information.	• It's easy to tell what the main idea is. • Most of the time the content is clear and focused. • There are some good details. • The reader still needs to figure things out.	• The main idea is well developed. • The content is clear and focused throughout. • The writing includes the right number of appropriate details.
ORGANIZATION	• There is no identifiable lead. • Transitions are missing. • The order of the details is random. • There is no ending; the writing just stops.	• There is a weak writer's lead. • Transitions are weak. • There is some order, but the writing is confusing. • There is a weak writer's ending.	• There is a writer's lead, but it could be better. • Transitions are repetitive and sometimes don't work. • At times the order makes sense, but not always. • There is a writer's ending, but it needs to be more effective.	• The writing has an effective writer's lead. • There are smooth transitions that make the writing easy to follow. • The order makes sense. • There is an effective writer's ending.
VOICE	• There is no voice, only information. • The writing is boring, stiff, and mechanical. • The writer doesn't seem to care about the topic or the audience.	• Sometimes there is voice, and sometimes there is just information. • The writing is distant, overly formal, or too informal. • The writer can't seem to hit the right tone.	• The voice is acceptable for the topic, audience, and purpose, but it doesn't bring the writing to life. • The writing is pleasant, agreeable, and satisfying. • Much of the time, the writer seems to care about the topic and the audience.	• The voice makes the writing come to life. • The writing is lively, expressive, and engaging, with lots of energy. • The writer really seems to care about the topic and audience, and it shows throughout the writing.

6-TRAIT WRITING ASSESSMENT RUBRIC

| Trait | More Weak Than Strong | | More Strong Than Weak | |
	Single (1)	Double (2)	Triple (3)	Home Run (4)
WORD CHOICE	• The words are not used correctly. • The writer uses limited and repetitive vocabulary. • The words are colorless and flat. They fail to communicate.	• Some words are used correctly. • Some verbs and nouns are strong, and some are ordinary. • There is an over-reliance on passive verbs. • The descriptions confuse the reader.	• Most of the words are used correctly. • Most verbs and nouns are strong. • The words get the job done, but the writing is not there yet. • At times, too much description buries the reader in details.	• The words are fresh and unique. They make the message clear and memorable. • There are strong nouns and lively verbs throughout. • The writer creates clear mental pictures through effective words.
SENTENCE FLUENCY	• The writing is really hard to read aloud. • The reader must stop and reread to get the meaning. • The reader cannot tell where sentences begin or end because of run-ons and/or fragments.	• Most of the sentences begin the same way and are the same length. • At times, the writing has to be reread to get the meaning. • There are still inappropriate fragments and/or run-on sentences that interfere with flow.	• The writing can be read aloud but lacks enough rhythm and flow. • Some sentences begin in different ways and are different lengths but are still basically simple sentences. • In general, if there are fragments, they are used for a purpose.	• The writing is a joy to read aloud. • The sentences vary in length and structure. • Sentence structure, rhythm, and flow match the purpose. • Fragments are used effectively.
CONVENTIONS	• There are errors that interfere with meaning. • No attention is given to capitalization, agreement and usage, punctuation, spelling, or paragraphing. • Much editing would be needed before this writing would be publishable.	• There are errors that detract from the meaning. • Some attention is given to capitalization, agreement and usage, punctuation, spelling, and paragraphing. • Moderate editing would be needed to make this writing publishable.	• Some errors are present, but they do not detract from the meaning. • Reasonable attention is given to capitalization, agreement and usage, punctuation, spelling, and paragraphing. • Light editing would be needed to make this writing publishable.	• The errors are so few that the reader can read right over them. • Capitalization, agreement and usage, punctuation, spelling, and paragraphing are all excellent. • The writing is virtually ready to publish.

Print Resources

Calkins, Lucy McCormick. *The Art of Teaching Writing*. Rev. ed. Portsmouth, NH: Heinemann, 1994.

Chicago Manual of Style, The. 15th ed. Chicago: The University of Chicago Press, 2003.

Culham, Ruth. *6 + 1 Traits of Writing: The Complete Guide* (Grades 3 and Up). New York: Scholastic, 2002.

————. *Using Picture Books to Teach Writing with the Traits*. New York: Scholastic, 2004.

Culham, Ruth, and Amanda Wheeler. *40 Reproducible Forms for the Writing Traits Classroom*. New York: Scholastic, 2003.

————. *Writing to Prompts in the Trait-Based Classroom: Content Areas*. New York: Scholastic, 2004.

————. *Writing to Prompts in the Trait-Based Classroom: Literature Response*. New York: Scholastic, 2004.

Diederich, Paul B. *Measuring Growth in English*. Urbana, IL: National Council of Teachers of English, 1974.

Fletcher, Ralph, and JoAnn Portalupi. *Writing Workshop: The Essential Guide*. Portsmouth, NH: Heinemann, 2001.

Forsten, Char, Jim Grant, and Betty Hollas. *Differentiated Instruction: Different Strategies for Different Learners*. Peterborough, NH: Crystal Springs Books, 2002.

Frank, Marjorie. *If You're Trying to Teach Kids How to Write . . . You've Gotta Have This Book*. Rev. ed. Nashville, TN: Incentive Publications, 1995.

Lane, Barry. *The Reviser's Toolbox*. Shoreham, VT: Discover Writing Press, 1998.

Marzano, Robert J., Debra J. Pickering, and Jane E. Pollock. *Classroom Instruction That Works: Research-Based Strategies for Increasing Student Achievement*. Alexandria, VA: Association for Supervision and Curriculum Development (ASCD), 2001.

Olness, Rebecca. *Using Literature to Enhance Writing Instruction: A Guide for K–5 Teachers*. Newark, DE: International Reading Association, 2005.

Spandel, Vicki. *Creating Writers Through 6-Trait Writing Assessment and Instruction*. 4th ed. Boston: Pearson, 2005.

Web Sites

www.crystalsprings.com	Crystal Springs Books
www.sde.com	Staff Development for Educators
www.greatsource.com	Great Source
www.nwrel.org	Northwest Regional Educational Laboratory
www.DTJudy.com	Discovery Toys
www.zaner-bloser.com	Zaner-Bloser

Index

Boldface page references indicate reproducible material.